W0017879

BUILDING A
BETTER
RUNNER

Science-Based Training for
Peak Performance

BUILDING A
BETTER
RUNNER

Science-Based Training for
Peak Performance

TERRY HAMLIN

Vertel Publishing
Charleston, SC

Building a Better Runner
Copyright © 2019 by Terry Hamlin

All rights reserved
No portion of this book may be reproduced, stored in a retrieval system, or transmitted in any form by any means–electronic, mechanical, photocopy, recording, or other–except for brief quotations in printed reviews, without prior permission of the author.

First Edition

Printed in the United States

ISBN-13: 978-1-64112-014-2
ISBN-10: 1-64112-014-2

To the love of my life, Dolly Hamlin

and

To my dear friend Julian Smith,
The best Race Director I have ever known

special thanks to Madeleine Fink
for assisting me with the computer graphics

ENDORSEMENTS

Terry is a man who knows running. He was on the leading edge of the running boom. And it was well known in the Charleston area that if you needed information about running, he was the man to talk to. Terry was President and Founder of The Charleston Running Club, when Dr. Marcus Newberry was thinking about organizing a race over the Cooper River Bridge. Terry was asked to help Dr. Newberry create the race. He is in the Cooper River Bridge Run Hall of Fame, has run the race, finishing in the top ten in the early 80's and has a 2:36 Boston Marathon.

It is easy to remember how well respected Terry was and is, in the running community. He has advised beginner to elite athletes for years. Terry organized the first Women's Only race in the state of South Carolina. This was before TAC/USATF standards for race management. I watched him measure the entire 5k race course with a steel tape. Can you imagine pulling that tape and marking an out and back course? That's what he did. He wanted it to be an accurate course and made sure it was.

So, if you are thinking, 'why should I listen to what he says in this book?', there should be no question he knows what he is talking about. Terry has been there and done that. This is a book every runner should read.

Cedric Jaggers, Editor South Carolina Runners Gazette, author Charleston's Cooper River Bridge Run, a Complete History, 1978-2010.

I have known Terry for most of my adult life. He watched me develop into a national caliber college runner. Terry lives the sport. He has been a very high level runner and coach. He has an endless passion for the sport called running. He has studied the Lydiard system and the new information we have, as well. Who better to put it down in a book to pass his knowledge on to runners of all levels. I am very proud to endorse Terry Hamlin's new book.

Irving Batten, Deputy Race Director, Cooper River Bridge Run, coach, two time Marcus Newberry Award winner, Cooper River Bridge Run Hall of Fame, Charleston Southern University track and field/cross country Hall of Fame.

As an athlete, there are times when it is easy to get discouraged.... and even in those times we are still evolving. Coach Terry sets ambitious goals for his athletes, gives them guidance and makes them realize they are capable of things they never dreamed of. Running is not always full of PR's, but through the hills and valleys, Terry will remind you to enjoy the journey.

Hannah Moldenhauer, USATF Level 1 Coach.

Coach Terry Hamlin has spent years documenting what it takes to develop confident and capable athletes. This book shares the full breadth and scope of personal and environmental considerations necessary for men and women to start with even just an interest in running—and become a more informed and well-rounded athlete.

Matt Moldenhauer, triathlete, marathoner, PLA, ALSA, PMP.

FOREWORD

BY BILL RODGERS

I am very glad to endorse Terry Hamlin's new book. It has everything for the beginner to the experienced runner. We are in dire need of people who really know the sport. Terry knows it. He is a runner himself, and that goes a long way. Terry has run at a higher level than many, but understands the hobby runner to the elite athlete. He has taken hobby runners to the level of the Olympic trials, from their first miles as a method for fitness. He is a coach, having worked with hundreds of runners, and understands the physical state and the personality of those who want to be good runners but don't think of themselves as athletes. He knows how to work with those who may even have had a negative experience trying to improve as a runner. To become a good or great runner is hard to do, so you need the type of information and assistance this book contains.

General health and fitness for runners has never really been addressed in this sport. Terry delineates fitness from health and merges the two into a lifelong enjoyable pursuit.

All the biophysical changes we go through as beginner runners are in this book. I appreciate how Terry melds the hard data of cell science in athletes to the psychological benefits from gentle to hard running. If you love running, this book has everything. This simple "one foot in front of another" sport is amazing. Take advantage of this book to learn the sport from a true expert. Terry has gone from an able-bodied runner to an amputee runner , as the result of a freak farm accident, without missing a beat. He has incredible perspective and looks at the sport as not only a way to benefit inside and outside, but to assist the runner in looking and participating in the sport for a lifetime.

Bill Rodgers

Four-Time NYC Marathon and Four-Time Boston Marathon Winner

Deemed the Best Runner of the Twentieth Century, from the Ten-Thousand-Meter to the Marathon, by The Athletics Congress

Called the "King of the Roads" by *Sports Illustrated*

Twice Ranked Number One Marathoner in the World, by The TAC

Two-Time American Record Holder in the Marathon

INTRODUCTION

PLAY HAS A PURPOSE

Children are natural athletes. Play is a product of our evolution, to keep us "in the chase." The means of playing, in the child who has learned to walk, is in the form of running. Play is embedded in a child as a way to foster not only the ancient means to hunt and survive, but also as part of our socialization process. Play, in the adult, also keeps our ability to socialize and communicate physically, without words and speech. Many of us somehow lose this desire for play as our busy lives consume our hours and distract us from a necessary and healthy activity.

This book is a treatise on becoming and, indeed, achieving the runner you had no idea was in you. This is not a self-help book. This is a plan and program that has been used by the best runners on the planet to get to the top. You may not become an elite runner or Olympian, but you will improve beyond your expectations.

As a child, I played outdoors, constantly moving, running, swimming, and surfing. We all did. As I grew older, I realized many of the competitive team sports were not suited to my body type and mental focus. I believe I was born a runner. Many of you believe the same about yourselves. And you are right. You just do not know the way to become the best runner in you.

This is a long-term—indeed, a lifelong—program. It may change your life forever. Some will fail as well. Dedication to this endeavor is difficult. Therefore, the first thing to be addressed is the mind of the runner. The mind of the athlete who will not quit, who does not accept failure, and who believes the horizon is the finish line—the endgame we seek. So, this book is additionally a book on one aspect of happiness in life. Running and doing your best in all things is a large aspect of our intent in this writing. Enjoy it, and never quit.

Terry Hamlin

THE MODERN RUNNING BOOM

The late, great Dr. George Sheehan once said, "We are all an experiment of one." Dr. Sheehan was a running guru to millions of runners and a personal friend. He knew the modern era of running started with, among other things, Frank Shorter's winning the gold medal in the marathon in the 1972 Munich Olympics. This win brought immense excitement to the sport in America, as an American had not won this event for decades. Dr. Sheehan correctly perceived the modern era of running would produce great advancements in medicine and the science of human performance. We everyday runners would be the lab rats for this great experiment. I credit Dr. Sheehan's passion for the sport, along with Dr. Kenneth Cooper's research and publication on aerobic fitness and performance, as the spark for changing countless lives for the better.

As the sport matured, along came a challenger of incredible determination. His name is Bill Rodgers, and he wrote the foreword to this book.

Bill came back to the sport after a brief absence when he watched the Boston Marathon in the Massachusetts town he called home. He knew he could one day win the greatest marathon in the world. And after a couple of fits and starts, he sailed to a 2:09:55 win in 1975, wearing a hand-scrawled GBTC Track Club t-shirt. It shocked the marathon world once again to know we had the talent to run with the best. The running boom was well underway from Shorter's Olympic victory, but it was clear that running was destined to take many average hobby runners to new heights. Now, Bill was far from a hobby runner, having run under nine minutes for two miles in college. As the years passed, Bill and Frank dueled in the most famous races in the nation. But Rodgers had an "everyman" allure that inspired average runners to work harder and see exactly what was in there. Rodgers won four Boston Marathons, four New York City Marathons, and hundreds of other important races across the world, as well as being a teammate of Frank Shorter and Don Kardong in the 1976 Montreal Olympic marathon.

In 1979, Japanese National Champion Toshihiko Seko came to Boston to dethrone the great Rodgers at the Boston Marathon. Rodgers had been beaten by Seko at the Fukuoka Marathon, the equivalent of the Japanese National Championship. Rodgers was not one to take a beating, by even a great runner, lying down. Bill responded with a blazing 2:09:27 new American marathon record, soundly defeating Mr. Seko. When Rodgers toed the line, the bar was automatically set higher for the competition. *Sports Illustrated* featured him on the cover with the caption "The King of the Roads," and he indeed was. He had the longest streak of wins without a defeat ever achieved. The world had become whipped into a frenzy by these events and now took to this brutally difficult sport as if it were a secret potion of pleasure.

Knowing them, running against them (with futility, for the most part, I might add), and immersing myself in the running world created a love for the sport that has, at times, simmered as a failing candle and then blazed as brightly as a bonfire for over fifty years. It spurred me to create the great Charleston Running Club and cofound the even greater Cooper River Bridge Run, one of the largest 10k races in the world.

Therefore, this book is dedicated to the great Bill Rodgers; Olympic Gold Medalist Frank Shorter; the great Olympic gold medalist Joan Benoit Samuelson, my friend the late Dr. George Sheehan, the guru of running from the seventies to now; human performance researchers like Dr. Edward Fox; Dr. Kenneth Cooper of the Dallas-based Aerobics Institute; and the millions of my runner friends who search for the best within and never quit.

By the way, there is another statistic below about runners that was found during years of research by the best human performance scientists in the world. It was thought to be true even as far back as the sixties but subsequent research showed this to indeed be the case. I have certainly seen it in the runners I have known, and that number is in the thousands.

Curiously, runners, as a group, achieve at higher levels in all aspects of life. That fact doesn't surprise me. A human who is willing to take on the challenge of the marathon or the 5k doesn't generally accept failure in other areas of their lives. Their IQs tend to be higher, as well. It is not known if this is cause or effect, but it is interesting. We do know that aerobic exercise improves blood flow to all areas of the body, and that includes the brain, so it does make sense.

Hopefully, this book will ignite the spark or fan the flame in you. But it is not a book for the faint of heart. This book is a plan to make a good runner great and a great runner terrific. So, if you are willing to follow it, plan to excel. If you don't plan to follow it, put it down, as it will only collect dust.

WHY DO HUMANS RUN?

A SHORT HISTORY OF OUR DEVELOPMENT

Why is this section important in a book on distance running? To understand where we are seeking to go, we need to understand where we have come from and how we got here. Anthropologists generally accept that humans evolved from moving on four limbs to two. We didn't necessarily evolve from apes, as some believe, but we appear to be a completely different offshoot, as *Homo erectus* eventually became *Homo sapien* and the Neanderthal was a victim of survival of the fittest, though their DNA is still traced in many cultures.[1]

None of what is said in this book is meant to be controversial or religious or nonreligious. But one thing is certain about humans, and that is, we have much to continue to discover. I am absolutely convinced that becoming upright created a faster human, however, who could improve the quality of their diet. The ability to capture food animals added a more

---

1   Origins- Dr. Richard Leakey and Roger Lewin- E.P. Dutton, New York, NY-1977

high-quality amino acid complex and more varied fats for survival during times of less food and to help the female provide for the infant. This change developed more strength, higher cognition, and greater longevity in humans. The most ancient form of humans appears to have originated around the Rift Valley of Africa.[2] At least, this is the prevailing consensus of the archaeology and paleontology world so far. Humans have inhabited the area for over a million years and less developed primates, for even longer. Humans still move through the area, hunting, gathering, and simply commuting.

As the eons passed, the human form became more upright and leaner, faster, and more sociable, with longer legs and greater planning ability. Faster humans could catch more food, resulting in healthier bodies and an improved chance of infant survival. Humans, like other animals, have communication skills and have learned there is security and strength in grouping. Different groups assembled into tribes, thus adding more security and enhancing communication skills to other people. One group of Homo sapien moved out of Africa to the North, and at the same time there was another group of Homo sapien that originated in the Indo China region. This group moved West toward the middle Eastern area of Turkey and the surrounding regions, and also, this same Indo China man moved East toward the Pacific Islands and North, eventually crossing the Bering Strait about 30,000 to 50,000 years ago, into the North American Continent. The group moving

---

2   Origins- Dr. Richard Leakey and Roger Lewin- E.P. Dutton- 1977

out of the Rift Valley, migrated essentially North. At the same time, however, there was incredibly, a separate and yet identical DNA version of Homo sapien developing in Indo China. This group eventually spread West, intermingling with the African human and also migrated East, into what we now consider as Asia. From there, they moved across a land bridge of the early Bering Strait and down through North America about 30-50,000 years ago. These people we know as our Native Americans. The Pacific islands are populated by these same groups. It is truly wondrous that modern DNA studies can now connect these groups and help to age their migration patterns.[3]

Then there was the ancillary effect of becoming faster and more equipped to move and think. For, originally, we were not at the top of the food chain. There were other animals whose desire it was to make a meal of us. Being able to escape predators was a key factor in our survival as a species.

As we adapted and became faster, we hunted and chased previously unavailable food animals for longer distances at higher speeds. This varied and improved our diets and helped us grow taller. As we grew taller and more efficient, our surface-to-mass ratio became greater, and our weight became adapted to long-distance running for survival and hunting. Now, we could cool our bodies better during long, hot chases, and we moved closer to the top of the food chain. Thus, the runner was here to stay.

---

3   Who We Are and Where We Came From- Dr. David Reich- Pantheon Books- Random House-2018

As our brains developed, culture, tribes, and speech came about as a way to communicate, socialize, and plan. To prepare young humans to hunt, play developed and is with us still today. Play, in its many forms, is the result of preparation to hunt, though it is not necessarily critical to our survival now. However, it is seen in nearly all higher forms of mammals—including dogs, cats, squirrels, and horses—all types of social animals, and even down to lower forms of life. Play also improves communication, strength, and socialization. Our body is a miracle of complex chemical reactions amassed into an incredible form with intricate problem-solving ability, and it is, in my humble opinion, a gift from above. We contemplate our existence, search the stars, work, fight, and play. All of this has a purpose. For all our shortcomings, humans are fascinating. And one of the most interesting parts of this fascinating animal is our desire to compete and improve. Hence, we have the reason for this book's existence.

As we evolved, the modern man, *Homo sapien*, interbred and became more upright. Body type and muscle groups became more sophisticated. Slow twitch or endurance fibers developed to carry us long distances, and fast twitch fibers developed for speed, to get us there more quickly. Tribes of socialized groups teamed up to combine effort, and we learned how to hunt, herd, farm, and in addition to previous gatherer knowledge, we began to form villages, then towns and cities. One downside, unfortunately, of this socialization was the need to control "turf." Competition for food led to warrior groups and battles to control food-producing areas and provide buffers from opposing groups. Warriors needed to be fast and strong, use the best weapons, and be able to think on their feet. Thus, the earliest "training" to win came to the fore. The Romans are a good example of what strategy, fitness, and desire to win over all enemies and territories can produce in a human. The morality of conquering others through fighting is not what we are here to decide, though. And it wasn't just the fighter with the best tools who won. It was the man or woman who absolutely refused to lose as well. And that is, indeed, what we will address. Competition was inevitable. Hence, along came the first competitive long-distance runners.

The training system used here is an indirect result of how men and women became athletes due to the need to survive. Be it the miler or the marathoner, both need the same system of training, just in different ratios and speeds. The science of becoming the best runner possible is pretty much established now. We have had the basic knowledge for some time. What has been lacking is the assimilation of different aspects of training into a cogent schedule package, with the reasons for these schedules explained, as to make sense of the workouts. Diet will be addressed only as to how different fuels are assimilated and absorbed for use and the necessity of certain nutrients for better performance in endurance sports. Dietary expertise cookbooks and nutrient concentration will, however, be recommended. The avoidance of injury will be addressed, and the accepted therapies for recovery in the unfortunate event one suffers an injury will be included in more depth.

The fine line between being too rested and too fatigued is very important. No matter how informative a book may be, it is the athlete's responsibility to learn to read his or her body. There are age, genetic makeup, consistency, and duration of training issues that can only be accepted by the athlete himself or herself that will affect the effectiveness of this training system, naturally. But every person who chooses to maximize their ability to become the best they can be will experience some or a lot of success. This is the guide. You are the facilitator.

THE EARLY COMPETITORS

Running originally developed, as previously noted, to ensure survival. But as communities and towns became more preferred places to survive, trade, and learn, the natural inner competitor came into play. Leaders, tyrants, and the general citizenry used athletic competition as a way to establish rank in society and display power. But it was not just about political power. Athletes became the heroes of the community while, at times, making war to establish the top tier appear a less attractive option for opposing groups to consider. This notion of competition is apparently genetically encoded in animals.

Movement, feats of strength, and performing at a higher level than the norm was coming together all across the globe at the same time as socialization became more common. I do not believe, and I think most modern anthropologists do not feel either, that this was a coincidence. Religion or belief in a higher power is not thrown into the mix here, as I (and this opinion is mine) firmly believe there is no coincidence in the universe and there is a higher power that brings order to the direction and development of man. Whether the reader accepts or denies any of this statement is personal, however, and has no discussion here on the science of training.

So, let's pursue this treatise as it pertains to established scientific methods of becoming a better athlete. Belief has helped me, but your thoughts on this are your own. Here is an idea of how many different groups eventually seized upon this beautiful sport and the inner freedom it brings.

THE AFRICANS

As was earlier mentioned, modern man is believed to have developed in Africa, as far as we have currently established, in the central valley and northern areas we call the Rift Valley and near Morocco. There is new evidence that modern humans and Neanderthals interbred in some areas, and there was also an Indo China component of the development of modern man. The research and archaeology in the area supports the developmental theories of man on four legs to man on two and then man upright becoming leaner and faster, with increasing endurance capability. The human body adapts to its environment, be it extremely cold, as in the Eskimo natives of northern climates, or extremely hot, as in the Rift Valley. As the Africans developed and became stronger, they spread out across the continent and differing climates made it important to tune the body as efficiently as possible.

There is now evidence, pointed out in the work of Dr. David Reich of Harvard University, that initial migration of man was north to the Northern Europe areas and an east-to-west migration from Indo China, as well as an eastern migration of these peoples to the Pacific Islands and north to the Siberian Peninsula.[4] Central Africans have more stout bodies than East Africans. The East African areas of Kenya, Ethiopia, Nigeria, Somalia, and the surrounding lands around Egypt and Morocco and down through the Rift area produced an incredibly well-suited climate and terrain to develop the distance runner's body. The heat and necessity to traverse long distances to find food and water improved these individuals into virtual running machines. High surface area to body mass, high VO2 (volume of oxygen the body is able to uptake and utilize, per breath) uptakes from living at altitude, and the mental ability to stay after the prey for miles and miles made them the prototype distance runner we think of today. They are always a force to be reckoned with in races from the mile to the marathon.

More stout African bodies developed in the Congo region and in the Central African jungle areas for the necessity of strength to avoid lethal attacks from incredibly strong prey.[5] Sometimes the human was the prey, so strength and great bursts of speed were needed to avoid death. Hence, they developed more fast twitch or 'speed' muscle fiber. Their bodies today represent the fabulous sprinters we see. Athletics allow us to see us as we were developed, as well as what we do now

---

4   Who We Are and Where We Came From- Dr. David Reich- Pantheon Books-
     Random House-2018
5   The Mountain People- Colin Turnbull- Simon and Schuster- 1972

for play and work. And the African athlete represents us many times at our best as determined and physically strong and developmentally darn near as good as we get.

THE GREEKS

The ancient Greeks developed out of Northeast Africans mingling with Western Europeans and migration to more ambient environments. The Greeks then intermingled with lighter skinned humans from cooler environs. As they evolved and socialized with additional groups developing to the East, they let the natural desire to compete out and utilized competition to showcase the best warriors and hunters, rewarding them with status in society. Most know the story of the Greek General Miltiades giving a warrior the task of running the plains of Marathon to Athens after a victory in battle against Persian invaders and collapsing in death after delivering the news. This is where we get the name of our 26.2 mile race, called the Marathon. The Greeks are also credited with the creation of the Olympics, to impress leaders and make sure other cultures knew who they were dealing with. Running, wrestling and other games of strength and skill were appreciated by the public and the games gave them a way of becoming involved, through spectatorship or participation. These games had another effect, as well. They substituted for actual battle and relieved the pressure valve of aggression inherent in humans and most animals.

The games died out for a time, as societies rose and were defeated and once again, war shifted the public's attention to surviving. The Celts' migration into Northern Europe about three thousand years ago, helped keep competition alive, as each group sought to prove its mettle. This wasn't just happening in Europe. It was happening in Africa and Mongolia and in the early Americas, as the native population created games amongst themselves to pass the time and once again, showcase superiority and substituting competition for war.

THE VIKINGS

As time passed, Nordic society came into prominence, through conquering societies in what is now Scotland, Ireland, England and even further south. They are mentioned here for several reasons. The Vikings lived in the harsh areas of Northern Scandinavia. Many think of the Vikings as just plunderers and pillagers, but they were indeed, different than Hollywood has portrayed them. They were skilled farmers, sailors, ship builders and created some of the most intricate metal and precious stone adornments ever seen. Their gold, stone and gem decorative jewelry is still today, thought of as some of the finest produced in the history of man.[6] But, like many, they were also opportunists and sought to increase their lands and riches through defeating those of less power. Their environs had

---

6   The Vikings- Gwyn Jones- Oxford University Press, UK- 1984

developed a tall, strong statured human who struck fear into the small villages and encampments, as their sails appeared on the horizon.

The Vikings also had athletes. They developed the term we now know as 'berserk' from the warrior athletes they called (Berserkers). These fearless fighters were the first line in battle, perhaps because of their wild rage, probably brought on as an alcohol fueled frenzy. They drank a grain based alcoholic drink called mead, which no doubt helped their bravery and near immunity to pain. The appearance of a Viking ship bearing down on a village, struck enormous fear into hearts of those they attacked. But, they also competed among themselves, with throwing, hand to hand combat and running.[7] The Nordic runner we see today is a direct descendant of the Viking. Many are tall and had great muscle mass. But, as food became more plentiful and muscle mass and high body fat became less important, running became more of a way to traverse the mountainous regions of Scandinavia and Northern Europe. The Scandinavian runner developed higher surface to mass ratios, as discussed in the introduction of this book and some became the 'Fell Runners', discussed in the next section. These were distance running machines. Higher muscle mass was retained however, in some of these tribes. We see that in Nordic and Germanic male and female strength athletes today. The Northern European female shot putters and high jumpers are incredibly well suited to their sport. And the tall,

---

7   The Vikings- Gwyn Jones- Oxford University Press, UK- 1984

lean Scandinavian athlete is epitomized in the famous Finnish runner Lasse Viren, winner of multiple Olympic medals, whose mental and physical toughness and refusal to lose, is the true mark of the Viking spirit.

THE NATIVE AMERICANS

It is believed the Americas were settled as a result of migration of Eastern Mongolian tribes across a strait in the upper Bering Sea during the early part of the last ice age, which lowered sea levels and exposed a land bridge into North America, perhaps as early as thirty to fifty thousand years ago. The actual timeline verdict is still out, as earlier and earlier settlements continue to be discovered in the Americas. However, the point here is the action of the inhabitants. The great American native hunters chased buffalo, elk, mastodon and other large, fast and powerful food animals and the games developed by these societies were a reflection of their preparation of youth to survive. Games of running, throwing and high endurance and strength challenges made for another group of great athletes. The Native Americans in the Northern and Southern areas of the continent were also extremely creative, artistic, spiritual and developed methods of farming, such as terrace farms on hillsides that are used to this day. They also were, as the Egyptians, incredible builders of pyramids and fortified cities. In modern times, we bring to mind the great Lakota Sioux tribe member, Billy Mills, winner of the gold medal in the

1964 ten thousand meters in the Tokyo Olympics. Billy Mills brought the gold medal to America in the Olympic 10k for the first time and brought enormous pride to Native Americans of all tribes, as well as all others in the nation. His incredible 'come from behind' win, is well documented and the event and his life prior to and after, was illustrated in a movie of his life.[8]

Thus, we see the same patterns of survival developing sports across the world at roughly the same time period. The desire is there in every human. Some are merely suited more to one sport than another. But, it was running and our brain that got us here.

THE NORTHERN EUROPEANS

In the late 1960's, I read an article about a British gentleman named Josh Naylor. Josh was a "Fell Runner". Fell running is a sport created, as we have seen in many societies, from a necessity. Sheepherders in the British and Scottish highlands had to move their stock to their prime grazing areas and back into the highlands, according to the seasons and as not to deplete the grass sheep primarily fed on. These areas ranged from lowland bogs to high elevation mountain ranges, or "fells".

Herders had to be incredibly fit to move with the animals and keep them from harm. Herders became natural endurance athletes, though playing a sport was originally not the

---

8   The Indian Reporter- CaliforniaIndian Education.org

purpose of their activity. They had to be able to walk and run, sometimes up to a hundred miles on high, unstable footing and ancient trails. Eventually, an informal sport developed among these men, to see who could cover these incredible distances, under all environmental conditions, in the shortest time. As you will see, endurance running has been around since we could stand. The Roman Centurions had a huge effect in the European theater. Their battles to claim lands from Scotland to the Mideast demanded the development of an endurance trained, Spartan type of human. These warriors were trained from birth to do this job. An offshoot of this development and fighting came to the fore in the creation of the term we use for the 26.2 mile race we call the 'Marathon'. It is said a warrior ran actually about this distance as a courier to report on the outcome of a battle near the plains of Marathon and that is now the name of this race distance. Today, running and track and field is still extremely popular in the area from Ireland down to England and I believe this was part of this endurance heritage born out of an unpleasant part of history.

SO HOW DOES THIS MACHINE WORK?

TRAINING EFFECT

All improvement for athletes is based upon increasing sessions of repetitive, increasing workloads, followed by appropriate rest periods. The result of this repetition is a biological response on the sub-cellular level. This is called 'training effect'.

The cellular changes that occur produce a muscle that can respond faster and longer, without building an overload of lactic acid, the chemical that slows the muscle up, yet can also be reconverted to a source of energy through glycolysis. Lactic acid, in this situation, is a protective mechanism. As workloads increase the cell structure undergoes biochemical changes. These changes are a way for the muscle cell to cope with the need for more fuel, the processing of oxygen and the elimination of excess lactic acid. An important change resulting from long term training is the cellular response of the creation of more mitochondria within the cell. Mitochondria can be thought of as the fuel containers or batteries of the cell.

They also serve to make the above chemical changes happen. The result is an increase in the cell of myoglobin and hemoglobin in the blood to utilize available oxygen more quickly and in higher amounts, while converting adenosine diphosphate to adenosine triphosphate, which is liberated as energy when a mole of phosphorous is broken off, with CO_2 eliminated as waste and water eliminated through expiration and the skin. Water may be one of the offshoots of burning fuel, but it mostly exits through the skin, helping to cool the body. Fuel, in the form of food, is consumed along with fluids generally and they are both equally necessary for not only sport, but survival itself. Carbohydrates are broken down for use in the form of glycogen. Fats and protein are broken down and are important as both fuel and rebuilding of the muscles and bones that are worn down. Energy in the cell when using glycogen, the most accessible fuel, occurs as a mole of inorganic phosphorous is broken off the molecule of ATP (adenosine triphosphate). Fats are also accessible for fuel, but require, as we shall see, more oxygen to liberate the fuel or 'burn' it. Protein can also be a source of energy, but the body will burn glycogen first, fats second and protein last, even though fats take more oxygen to liberate as fuel. When the body has resorted to burning proteins, it means there will be a breakdown of muscle tissue, so the body uses the least destructive forms of fuel first. This all sounds complex, but the simple, net effect of training is that the body adapts to become more efficient and is able to use more oxygen from the blood stream. The human body is truly remarkable. As stress is applied during work in the form of walking, running or lifting, our bodies do not remain molecularly or cellularly static. Training effect means the body changes to adapt itself to the extra workloads we put it through during exercise. Gradually increase the work-load, rest and repeat, with extra caloric intake and the body becomes a more and more efficient machine.

THE BASIC CELL

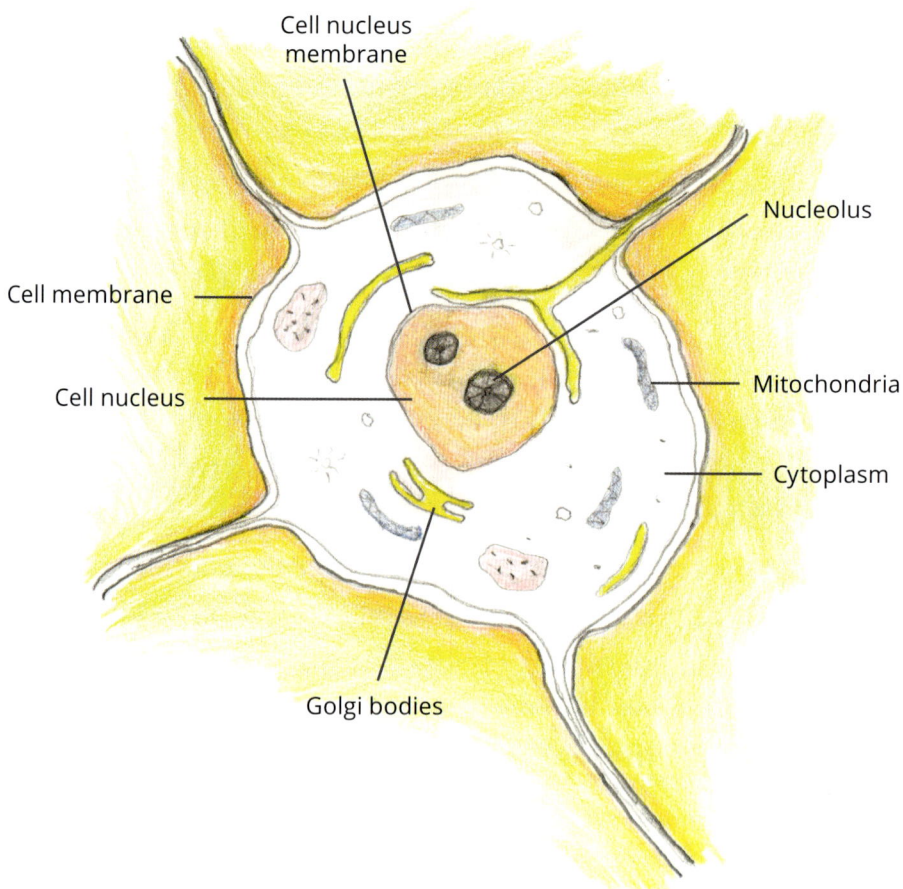

Note the difference between this untrained cell and the trained cell on the following page. A higher level of mitochondria provides more energy storage.

THE TRAINED CELL

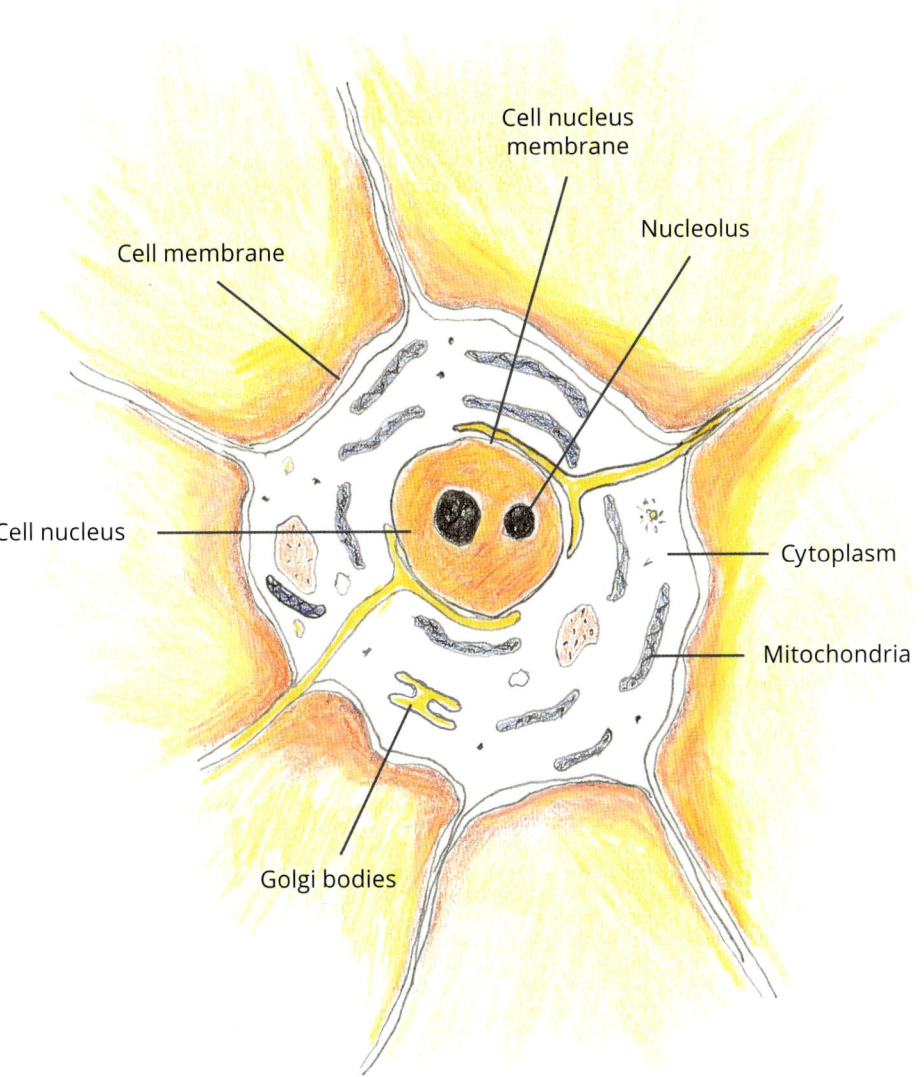

Cell nucleus membrane

Nucleolus

Cell membrane

Cell nucleus

Cytoplasm

Mitochondria

Golgi bodies

Note the higher number of mitochondria, which results in a stronger cell with additional ability to provide energy.

THE DISTANCE RUNNER PROTOTYPE

To traverse long distances at high speeds, several physiological factors are helpful. First, since it takes more oxygen and energy production to move higher mass, a lighter body weight is helpful. Second, running higher mileage over several years to develop maximum VO2 is absolutely necessary. Running the higher mileage usually accomplishes the first point, a reduction in mass, as body fat is reduced due to expending glycogen stores to the point that fat must become a bigger component of fuel burned. Next, good flexibility is important, to increase stride length and reduce the incidence of muscle tear. The fewer strides one has to take covering a 5k or a marathon, the greater speed that may be achieved. Beware of the urge to over stride, however. If the foot hits the ground ahead of the shoulder, chest, hip and knee straight line, the runner will have to overcome a 'braking' effect. This will be addressed in the section on form.

The elite runner will possess another important factor. A correct ratio of slow twitch fiber, which uses oxygen as its primary source of fuel conversion and transport, to fast twitch fiber, which is much less dependent on oxygen, is found in all top level distance runners.[9] The oxygen in this mechanism is not a part necessarily of the chemical reaction, but is important in the survival of the cell and is part of the waste product in the form of CO_2 and H_2O expelled from the lungs and skin after the fuel conversion has occurred. Long Distance runners tend to have a ratio of 80% slow twitch (aerobic) to 20% fast twitch (anaerobic) fiber within the muscles. Sprinters, on the other hand need explosive energy, utilized through the lactic acid or anaerobic system from fast twitch fiber. Great sprinters have almost an opposite ratio of about 80% fast twitch to 20% slow twitch fiber. We will explore that somewhat, but we are concerned more with the development of the slow twitch fiber primarily and the fast twitch fiber secondarily, as the necessary muscle component mix for high level distance runners. And this cannot be stressed enough. The body must have the aerobic systems, with increased mitochondria, higher levels of myoglobin, hemoglobin and the ability to utilize fuel, oxygen and handle lactic acid all properly trained, before moving into the strength and speed phase. This Distance Training Phase is both cause and effect in producing a proper distance runner's body. The basic shape of elite runners starts with a semi-ectomorph (lean) shape. The mesomorph (average weight) and

---

9   Sports Physiology- Dr. Edward L. Fox- Saunders College Press- 1977

endomorph (heavier) body type can be molded into a very good runner, but some of these higher mass body types will be better suited for other sports if they want to achieve elite levels of performance, simply because it takes more energy to move more mass.

So what is the ideal physical design of the high level distance runner? In males (and females will also be addressed), he is usually from 5'5" to 5'11" in height. His weight ranges from 115 pounds in the shorter males, up to approximately 150 pounds in the taller men. His body fat ratio is as low as 1.5% to a high of 3-4%. He has a longer leg to trunk ratio, meaning he can take long strides easily, with lower output of energy. His O2 uptake is extremely high due to training and can reach 80ml/kg/min absorption, as opposed to normal respiration in untrained humans, of 38ml/kg/min. So, we see that consistent training is causation for adaptation to incredible levels of endurance[10]. The endurance runner is a high powered engine in a light frame, just like a race car. By following this program, many will achieve much higher levels of performance.

The female distance runner is chemically similar to the male, but with a couple of evolutionary differences. She is a shorter height, with wider hips for child bearing. Female elite runners tend to range from just under 5 feet tall to 5 feet 10 inches tall and they will have a typical weight of 90 pounds or less and a high of 120 pounds. The human female carries

---

10   Sports Physiology- Dr. Edward L. Fox- Saunders College Press- 1977
      The Hidden Mechanics of Exercise- Christopher M. Gillen-The Belknap Press of
      Harvard University- 2014

more fat than the male, due to the responsibility of females to have and help infants survive. This was established eons ago, as a way for survival of infants and mothers until the offspring could find and consume food on their own. They carry higher levels of fat in their breasts, their hips are wider and their gluteus maximus has a bit more fat, presumably for use as fuel in times of famine, during our early development. Therefore, they start with a different ratio of fat to muscle. They usually have over 6% to 12-15% fat in taller females. Untrained females will have more fat, as they presumably are much more efficient in storage, even to this day. This is not a critique, but a fact of development. The female will dissipate heat slightly differently from males and they have, of course, different levels of testosterone and estrogen from their male counterpart. In males, weight tends to start falling with higher levels of training, very quickly. Females lose fat more slowly and retain higher natural levels for the above stated reproductive reasons. Therefore, females appear to store and metabolize fats more efficiently. In females however, their actual body weight may increase temporarily at the onset of distance training as they reduce the size of fat cells, but gain muscle. Muscle weighs more that fat, hence the reason for this sometimes 'alarming' revelation. There is no need for the female athlete to be concerned, however. And they should not decrease their caloric intake, as a response to this increase. They will begin to reduce weight after a section of distance training that takes them over 40-50 miles per week for six to eight weeks has occured They will start to achieve ideal body mass as their mileage increases, just as males do, only a bit more slowly. I add these comments because this concern consistently comes up in new female athletes I train. Even female elite milers have higher mass to height ratios[11]. The oxygen uptake in females is slightly lower, due to their smaller chest cavity and lungs. But, there is a curious advantage to be had particularly, by female ultra-distance runners. Presumably because they may be more efficient at shifting from glycogen to fat as a fuel, they can be incredibly strong ultra-marathon runners. Females have even outrun equally trained males in these 50 kilometer and longer, races. The other chemical conversions are exactly the same as the male. Of course, females have different levels, as noted, of hormones and perhaps they have a more efficient operation of the hypothalamus. This may be part of the various clues and questions as to the great performance of trained female runners. The female runner in an elite level of training will have a VO2 uptake similar to males. They will go to 60-80ml/kg/min uptake, just as the elite male distance runner. So, even though they have a smaller capacity, the uptake ratio when mass is considered, is every bit as efficient as a human with more actual muscle.

One thing that may occur in the high mileage elite female runner, however, is a hormonal change resulting in a lessening or even stopping, of monthly menstrual cycles during high level training. Note that this is not an across the board effect in females as they lose fat, by any means. No one is completely

---

11   Sports Physiology- Dr. Edward L. Fox- Saunders College Press- 1977

certain of the reason for this, although many scientists believe the reduction in body fat is tied to this cycle and it therefore, is a protective mechanism in females, to prevent pregnancy in a female who may be in caloric distress. And not all high mileage female runners will necessarily experience this. It appears to be a temporary situation and according to current research, there appears to be no issue with pregnancy in women after this and cycles return to normal when training lessens and fat ratios go back up slightly.

One other issue females in particular should monitor is the possibility of hemoglobin deficiency, due to the natural female cycles. The binding of hemoglobin to oxygen for delivery to the muscle cells is extremely important, when considering the ability of an endurance athlete to perform or to even become anemic. If hemoglobin levels are lowered too far, iron is decreased while serum plasma has increased. Plasma volume is increased in all endurance athletes, therefore the ratio of hemoglobin and HbO2 (Hemoglobin binding), must parallel if the athlete is to avoid anemia. And females must be keenly aware of their levels of hemoglobin, hematocrit (percentage of red blood cells) and iron. This situation can also occur in males, by the way. Of course, your physician is the professional to consult if this issue arises. Physicians can run blood tests to establish whether these and other blood components are at normal levels. If levels are too low, changes in diet or even supplements may be added to raise levels to acceptable levels.

We do see another expected change. The hemoglobin and myoglobin levels in both the male and the female will be significantly higher in endurance athletes than the sedentary human, as a ratio, not necessarily as a static figure. Hemoglobin transfers oxygen to the cells from the alveoli of the lungs and myoglobin helps to make the oxygen available for use. Since much more oxygen is required to fire off the cells, this is normal.[12]

An Important Note on Body Mass in Runners and Proper Training Nutrition:

As has been described in the prototype of the elite or even the good distance runner, reduced body mass and therefore, weight, is lower in these athletes than in other sports. However, it is extremely important to not use this sport as a way to become a runway model. Anorexia can be somewhat associated with both males and females, when runners begin to see how lean they can become. This is a misuse of the intent of this sport and is medically dangerous. Elite runners covering up to 100 miles per week can burn an extra 10,000 calories a week. That alone, with no change in diet, can reduce weight by 3 pounds per week.

There becomes a negative effect associated with this when females fall below fifteen to percent body fat and males fall below three percent. Why the large range between the sexes? Females need more body fat to function physiologically, than males. They produce hormones at different levels than males,

---

12   The Hidden Mechanics of Exercise- Christopher M. Gillen-Belknap Press, Harvard University-2014

with more fat in the hips and breasts, but these hormones are there for more reasons than to just add curves. They help the female with protection and nurturing their infants, monthly hormonal changes, ovulation and therefore, a female can actually become infertile, develop more brittle bones, lose magnesium to dangerous levels and additionally, since many of both sexes now feel any amount of red meat with some measure of fat on it is bad, they both can become anemic. Make sure you are actually increasing caloric intake if you are losing weight too quickly. If you become too focused on weight loss, things can go bad. I know vegetarian distance runners, but they have to be careful to maintain proper hemoglobin levels, iron and B complex vitamins through means other than red meat. I personally, have absolutely no issue with red meat in reasonable amounts though most of the meat I personally consume is organically grown beef or more often, wild game like venison. Venison, elk and other wild ruminants are almost totally free of invasive antibiotics, artificial hormones and the like. They are also very low in fat and LDL cholesterol, making them a good choice for long term coronary health. Anyone, much less an athlete, cannot be too attentive to proper nutrition and meat or no meat, be sure to pay close attention to the proper intake of food and liquids, and their connection to good health. Doctor Ann Kulze is a highly trained physician and nutritionist and there is a list of her books on the subject at the back of this book. Pick up some of her books and experience the delicious recipes and huge amount of knowledge in this area, that Doctor Kulze provides. What you, as an athlete decide on this topic, is of your own choice. However, I have seen athletes actually die because they insisted on being too 'light' at the starting line, in order to give themselves an edge in training, a race or just in their overall body shape. I have also worked with a female physician who developed anorexia and eventually died. So, this is a serious issue that demands these statements. Be you female OR male, eat a good, balanced diet and don't overeat, but definitely do not skimp! Also, make sure you take in plenty of fluids in the form of water and/or some electrolyte replacement drinks. It takes approximately 4 grams of water to metabolize one gram of glycogen in the form of carbohydrates and the same ratio for protein, but it takes 9 grams of water to one gram of metabolize fat for energy! So, indeed do take in plenty of fluids with meals, before and during workouts and immediately after racing or training, as well as to cool the body through evaporative cooling and eliminating excess salts, mostly in the form of (NACL) or sodium chloride (table salt) and some magnesium (Mg). Replacing carbohydrates quickly after a hard training or racing session helps the body to recover more rapidly, as well. I find that mixing it up to a two to one or a three to one water to electrolyte replacement fluids, in the same size containers, is a good rule to follow and starting to intake complex carbohydrates along with fluids is helpful for recovery, especially when mileage gets high. Some runners have difficulty with sugary fluid replacement drinks and that is another reason to dilute the commercial drinks, if your stomach is sensitive. Plus, some drinks with high sugar content can slow absorption, making them less effective for rapid rehydration. If you (and this applies to males and females) are drinking enough fluids to make you urinate several times a day and eating properly, you are most likely on mark. If your urine is slightly bloody (males) and this is not temporary, see your physician. Occasionally, small capillaries in the bladder and ureter can break on hard training runs and produce a slightly bloody one-time urination. In females, monthly cycles can cause blood loss. In fact, this is a great reason for females to ensure they are including foods that build and maintain hemoglobin and iron levels.

As far as caloric level intake is concerned, it takes approximately 3,200 calories to equal a pound of body weight. We have mentioned this before, but females may actually increase their weight slightly as they move toward approximately 50 miles per week. This is NOT a function of increased fat. This is actually a great sign. It means muscle is being built. Muscle weighs more than fat, due to its higher density and composition. So, rather than becoming alarmed, females (and some males, as well) should recognize they are changing their body into a stronger, more efficient machine. When females cross the 50 mile per week line, they may see some reduction of mass or weight, as they are, in this respect, the same thing. This begins because they are now running long runs that utilize fat, as well as the usual glycogen, for fuel, particularly on runs that exceed eighteen miles. This 50 mile per week barrier is not a hard and fast line, but in the half a century plus experience of this writer, it has more often than not, been the mileage line at which runners undergo faster body shape and weight changes. There is no need to be alarmed at the lean look in this scenario if the athlete has taken in proper nutrition and calories as only excess or unnecessary mass is being reduced. Remember, it take less energy to move less mass. This weight loss occurs because, though we are actually burning a combination of glycogen and fat as we run. The body burns a much higher ratio of glycogen to fat, early in a run, though some fat is being utilized, even from the start. As the length of the run increases, the ratio must change, as glycogen is becoming depleted. The human body stores approximately 1,500kc of glycogen in the muscles and 500kc in the liver. One reason runners "hit the wall" at about twenty miles, is that glycogen, which as stated above, is much easier for the body to access and the transition to primarily burning fat after running through accessible glycogen, is more difficult and takes more oxygen. At about twenty miles and burning approximately one hundred calories per mile, the body makes a fairly rapid shift to using much more fat for fuel, as glycogen stores have been all but depleted. Hence, we train with long runs for several reasons, one of which is to train the body to access fat for fuel, by increasing our volume of accessible oxygen uptake in the lungs. If one has trained properly through the upcoming Distance Phase, more alveoli are created to absorb oxygen and the body has now created more transport systems and has increased cellular efficiency. The mass of the trained distance runner is lower, so with more long distance training, the 'engine' of the lungs will provide more accessible oxygen to the muscles and the athlete can run faster for longer periods.

I mention all of this to not only help the athlete to understand what is needed to supply the proper nutrients and density of fuels to run the body, but also for another important reason. The obsession with body shape in this nation (America) is creating a serious issue with the competition to be the 'lightest or skinniest' person in the crowd, particularly among females, but occasionally among males, as well. Anorexia and bulimia can and does, kill. Our weight loss should be coincidental to our sport, not a way to harm ourselves. There are very good treatment plans available to those who think they may have an issue with this. Listen to your friends and family, particularly your athletic friends. They may recognize unnatural weight loss before others, who may just expect weight to fall off.

Running is a great way to control weight, granted. But, it is not a great way to slowly commit suicide through lack of nutrients. If this statement sounds harsh, then I have gotten my message across. I monitor my athletes' weight. I don't do it every day and I actually encourage them to 'pig out' occasionally. A distance runner, or someone seeking to become a good distance runner, should enjoy all aspects of a good, healthy lifestyle, but not deny themselves a treat or two when they would like it. The human body is so incredibly and wonderfully wired, it will tell you when it has a need for some missing calories. As a young runner in my twenties, I ate nearly four thousand calories per day and still weighed below 140 pounds. So, do the work and you can eat the foods! But, this book is not a weight loss plan. It is a structured program to help runners achieve high levels of performance.

Now, here is one last 'preach' to the athlete/runner. Running increases the stroke volume of the heart, increases the size of the coronary arterial system, helps lower LDL cholesterol which is associated with heart disease development, while raising 'good' cholesterol HDL levels, increases the development of new capillaries within the muscles and ligaments and organs of the body, increases strength and oxygen efficiency, but it does not do one thing. It does not make us immune to death from heart or other disease. As you do all of this recommended training, remember the basics of a healthy life. Eat well, exercise consistently, keep alcohol intake low or non-existent, don't smoke (though I probably wasted those two last words) and get regular checkups from your physician. I met, but was not really friends with Jim Fixx. Jim wrote a great book on running for beginners in the 80's[13]. But, in all the great information Jim conveyed, there was at least in my opinion, an implied view that runners were nearly incapable of dying from lifestyle diseases. Unfortunately, Jim found out the hard way. Jim was thought to eat lots of fried foods and junk food, yet there was a history of heart disease in his family. Though Jim ran a lot of miles, one day it all came to an unfortunate end for a great man. Jim collapsed and died of a heart attack, while on a run. It was found he had major arterial plaque blockages, the cause of his fatal myocardial infarction. When blood flow

---

13   The Complete Book of Running- Jim Fixx- Random House- 1977

through the heart is interrupted, the accompanying electrical signals that control heart rhythm are disrupted, causing the heart to go into severe atrial fibrillation and/or shut down completely. This is what we call a 'heart attack'. So, take care of yourself. I abused my own body with this 'bulletproof' runner thinking and it also nearly caused serious physical problems, but I changed before issues got out of hand, fortunately. I want to go to your successful races and hear of your success stories due in part at least, to running, not your funeral.

So, what are the effects of distance running on the human body? The main changes we see are below.

Positive Aspects of Running

- Strengthen muscles

- Increase endurance

- Improve cardiovascular health

- Improves ability to sleep and to concentrate

Negative Aspects of Running

- Reduces flexibility

- Increases possibility of injury when improperly performed

- Increases muscle imbalance if core fitness is not incorporated

- Can cause a negative shift in socialization if training is not balanced with family and friend time

Faster Up and Faster Down

The physiological effects of training begin within 72 hours of the start of repetitive increases in workloads. More mitochondria are developed, hemoglobin and myoglobin levels begin to rise, the VO2 maximum uptake improves, more capillaries are added to muscles and the overall ability of the athlete to handle lactic acid and physical stress becomes more efficient. However, one interesting change that should not be ignored is that the increase in physiological efficiency begins to reverse by approximately 1% per day down to the original starting baseline, within 72 hours of becoming sedentary. So, in this training plan you will not see a recommendation to stop training completely for more than 48 hours, unless the athlete is

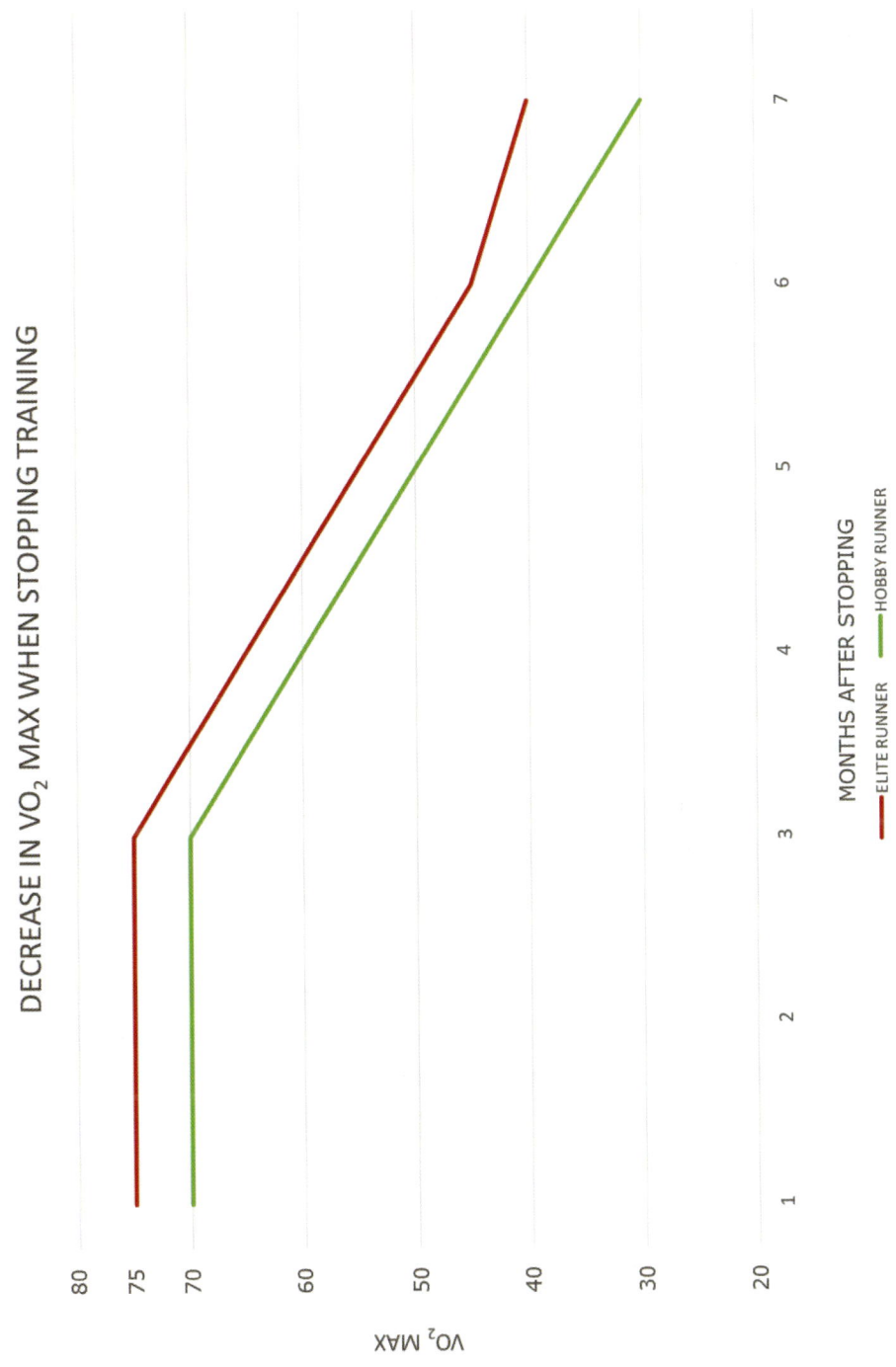

DECREASE IN VO₂ MAX WHEN STOPPING TRAINING

VO₂ MAX

MONTHS AFTER STOPPING

ELITE RUNNER HOBBY RUNNER

injured. Even then, there are usually rehabilitative exercises the athlete can utilize while healing that will reduce at least some loss of training effect. The estimated loss of VO2 gained uptake in an athlete who stops training is, as noted, approximately 1% per day after the 72 hour period, unless training resumes or supplementary aerobic exercise, like swimming or cycling for instance, is added to offset the reversal of increasing oxygen uptake and muscle strength. So the moral here is to rest properly, but this is what I meant by 'not too much'. The good news here is that an athlete will regain fitness more quickly after an injury or prolonged down time, than a sedentary person, due to acquired muscle memory.

The Hard/Easy Schedule

All great athletes use a form of the hard/easy schedule in their training to help maximize training effect. Consistently pounding the body day after day, only results in breakdown. There must be a period of rest in between each exercise session and increase in workload. The athlete is actually becoming more fit during the rest phase, ironically. Rebuilding cells and developing the mitochondria occurs during rest and after a hard exercise phase that has stressed the cell enough to trigger the biochemical changes previously discussed. As glycogen stores are replenished, ADP is converted back to ATP to become available for work again. Research has also shown that the more quickly glycogen and water and electrolytes are replenished, the faster the athlete will recover and systems brought up to maximum levels for hard training to resume. This applies to all who train, not just the elite athlete. A long run stresses the muscular system and oxygen uptake system at the same time. Continuously stressing the system without the rebuilding phase is a common mistake of new athletes. The body will break down if not given time to rest and rebuild. My athletes are always given an easy day after a very long run or hard speed work day. They maintain consistency while greatly reducing the chance of overtraining, by using this type of schedule. They may be running 100 miles per week and their long runs may be 22-23 miles, but an easy day of 8 to 10 miles should always follow the long day. If they are only at a long run of 10 miles, an easy day of 4 to 6 miles is in order for the next day. I always stress the fact that the athlete is actually building strength during the rest section between exercise performance workouts. Sleep is when we are rebuilding and actually getting stronger.

A Simple Guide to Measure Adequate Rest

There is a simple way to determining whether the athlete has rested enough between workouts. As the athlete improves and workload is able to increase, heartrate comes down during rest phases. For instance, a 'normal' resting heartrate in an untrained male may be over 60 beats per minute. In an elite distance runner, a resting heartrate may be under 35 beats per minute and can be as low as under 30 beats per minute. Establishing a baseline heartrate will help the athlete monitor

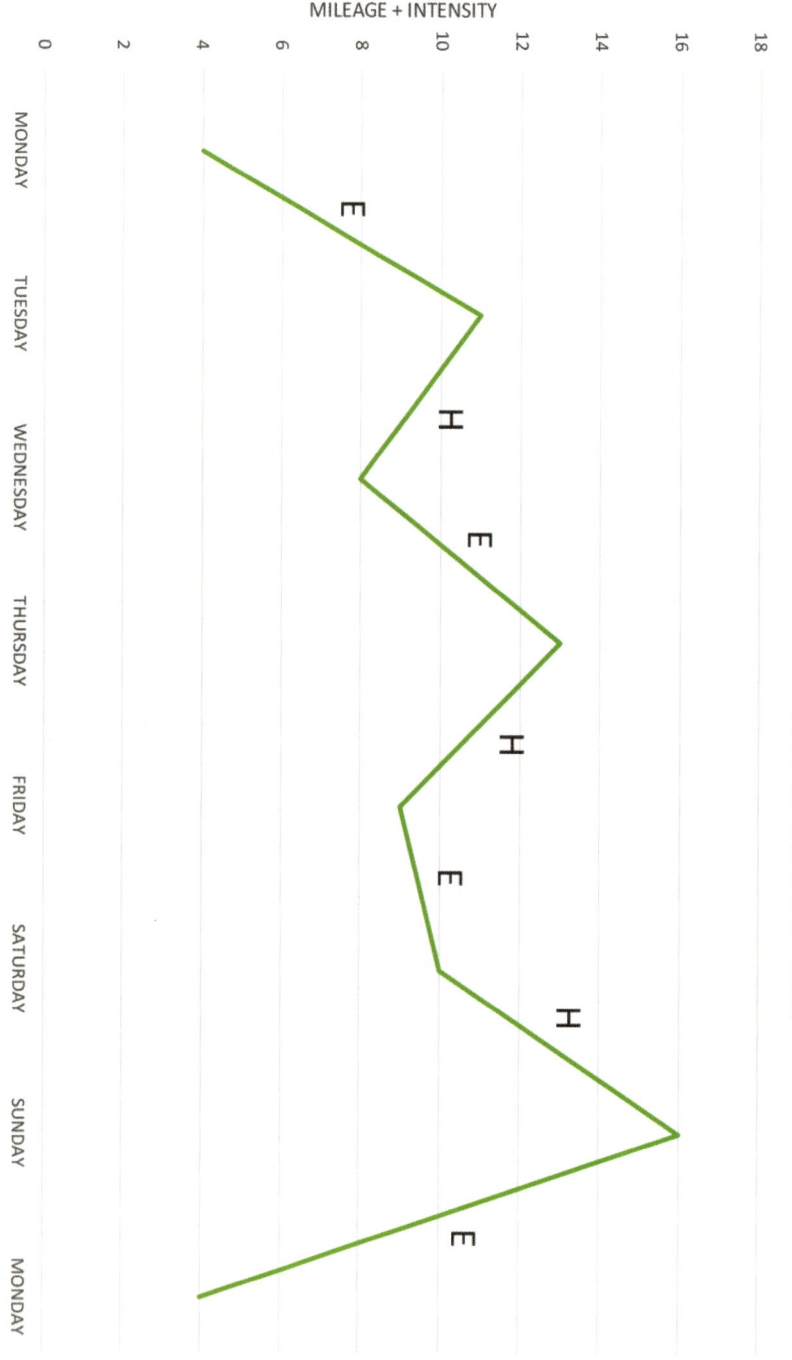

HARD/EASY SYSTEM: HOBBY RUNNER- DURING DISTANCE PHASE

E= INTENSITY LOW H= INTENSITY HIGH

whether the body is receiving proper rest between workouts. The following method is a great way to understand whether a rest day is needed.

Take your heartrate immediately upon waking each morning. Soon, a baseline average will be established. Initially, monitor your resting heartrate each morning for a week to establish the expected baseline level. Subsequently, if the resting heartrate is 10% higher than the normal baseline the morning after a hard workout, an easy day is advised, regardless of the day's schedule. An elevated heartrate indicates a body not yet recovered. Don't be afraid to give the body a break, when it is clearly asking for rest. Why does the resting heartrate come down in trained athletes and the maximum rate go up? As the body becomes more fit, the heart increases in size and pumping ability, particularly in the left ventricle. Therefore, each stroke provides more blood and thus, oxygen to the cells. The coronary arteries become larger to carry more blood with each stroke. Additionally, more capillaries develop to provide blood and oxygen more broadly to cells. There is an inverse relationship to the sedentary resting and the athletically trained heartrate. As the runner becomes more fit resting heartrate comes down, due to the increased stroke volume, while the ability to reach higher heartrates, increases. The actual size of the athletically trained heart also increases. Most of this increase comes from an increase in the large chamber of the left ventricle, which pumps oxygenated blood to the muscles. This, though described here in simple terms, is very accurate in measuring proper recovery time. Additionally, there is an ability to raise the maximum heartrate to higher levels and hold it there. That is what separates the trained, from the untrained body. Resting, in between training sessions, needs to be structured and as consistent as any workout. The next section describes a set of guidelines for ensuring proper rest during training and the race seasons.

Maximizing Recovery

As noted, recovery is a key to improvement. But how much is too much and how little is counterproductive? Rest can be defined in several ways. First, there is the resting of the physical organism. Second, there is the rest of the mind and emotions. Finally, there is the resting of the two, even during activity. We may think of rest as happening purely during sleep. And sleep is key and extremely important as the runner becomes more fit. But, there is rest that occurs even with light workouts. This is how the elite runner is able to achieve incredibly high mileage. The top elite runner covers 100 to 150 miles per week at times. How is this possible, while considering rest? Very simply, as the runner increases in fitness, the body is able to go into rest mode more easily and achieve better quality rest. The elite athlete still sleeps a minimum of 8-10 hours per night or more, but the rest is noted by researchers and physicians, as a better quality REM (rapid eye movement) sleep. Sleep typically falls into two phases during the night. The first phase of deep sleep is important to muscle tissue repair and the

RESTING HEART RATE

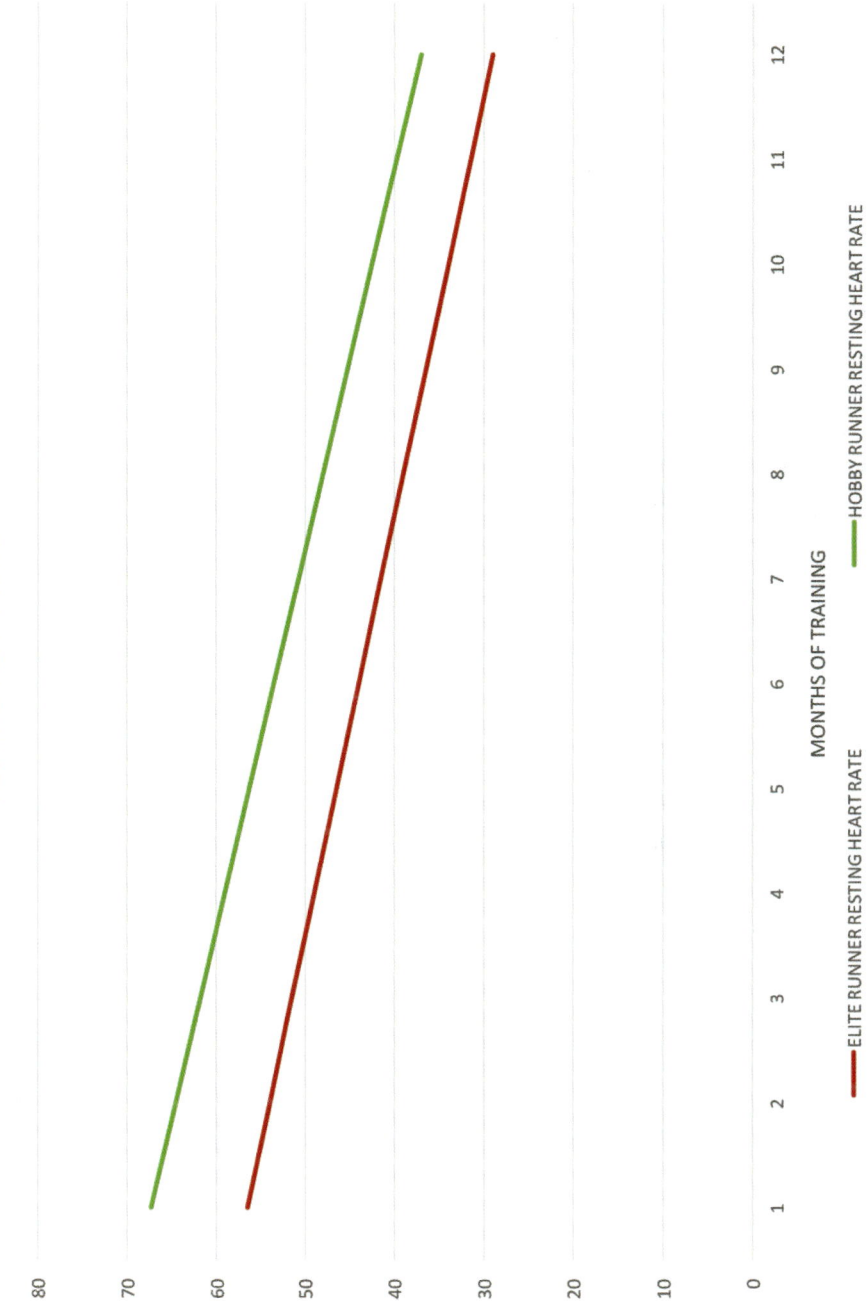

MONTHS OF TRAINING

RESTING HEART RATE: BEATS PER MINUTE

ELITE RUNNER RESTING HEART RATE

HOBBY RUNNER RESTING HEART RATE

formation of new tissue, needed for athletic improvement. The immune system benefits from this period of rest, as well. The second phase of sleep is marked by short, repetitive REM patterns. The psychological well-being and emotional health of an athlete who is highly endurance trained and under nearly continual repetitive physical stress, must rest well in order to regenerate the body, mind and immune health.

There is a pretty simple formula to determine whether the athlete is resting enough. During your entire year round training regimen, make a practice of taking your true resting heartrate, as described above. To do this, keep a journal or use your smartphone on your nightstand beside your bed and within arm's reach. As you awaken from sleep each morning, take your resting heartrate for 60 seconds. No phone calls or getting up before this is done. The runner who knows their body is better prepared to schedule the proper workout for the day and especially for the individual training sections leading up to the race season. Be sure to eliminate the morning readings taken after any early morning physical activity. If the athlete sees a pattern of resting heartrates that are 10% higher than normal, after establishing a baseline for approximately a week, then a rest day or even a couple of rest days, is needed.

The stress of high level physical training can temporarily damage muscle cells and capillaries, but proper sleep not only restores these cells and transport mechanisms, but also trains the body to handle harder training with less and less micro damage to these systems. Thus, the cell is rebuilding and adapting for the better, when we are at rest after the workout.

"The 'Alarmed Researcher' Story"

When I was running high mileage, I was asked to participate in a research program to determine whether a certain enzyme, (creatinine phosphokinase) that was thought to be a key to diagnosis of myocardial infarction (heart attack), would be elevated from hard running and rapid heartrate in a high level athlete, as it was in normal people who suffered such an event and if it would come from the heart or from the skeletal muscles. I wore a Holter-monitor for a week (a portable heartrate monitor and electrocardiogram instrument) twenty four hours a day, during exercise, rest and all other activities. This device records heartrate and rhythm constantly, twenty four hours a day. I was asked to do one of my normal, scheduled track workouts while wearing the device and a tube of blood was drawn after every third fast section. The workout called for a two mile warmup, stretching and then 16x400 meters at 70 to 71 seconds each, with a 125 meter recovery jog, in between each 400. The session was followed by a one mile cooldown and more stretching. It was discovered that my deep sleep heart rate was twenty seven beats per minute and my highest level achieved during the four hundred meter sprints at 4:40 mile effort, was two hundred and twenty-nine beats per minute. That is an incredible difference in the heart's ability to adapt and shows in real time, how training improves the efficiency and strength of the heart. Most fairly trained people at age twenty seven, (my age at that time), would have a resting rate during sleep, of fifty five to sixty beats per minute and the highest heartrate they would attain, would be approximately one hundred and ninety three beats per minute. In addition, blood was drawn from me during daily normal activity and during these intense exercise segments. It was found that the enzyme did increase very slightly in a trained athlete. But, this was found to be from the skeletal muscles and not the heart. However, I got a call from the lead cardiologist researcher a few days after the monitor was removed and read. He asked if I felt 'ok'. I said I felt great and asked why he was concerned. He said he had never seen heart rates this high or this low in a healthy individual. I commented to him that perhaps they should take a look at highly trained athletes as an entirely different group of humans, in terms of the performance of their bodies. Of course, a good deal of this was already beginning to be done by human performance scientists. But, as for this study, it was a shocking discovery. At least in this human, it proved that more highly trained athletes' bodies adapt in many ways, not just in oxygen absorption and ability to run fast.

THE PHASES OF TRAINING

As mentioned earlier, much of this training has been realized from such notables as Arthur Lydiard, Dr. Kenneth Cooper, Dr. Edward Fox and coach Bill Bowerman of Oregon among many others and they should be recognized for their early research and coaching methods. The basic four section "periodization" system, designed and used heavily by Lydiard, still works. It is in use by the best athletes, even today. However, we have added new information, as more research on athletes is done and the acceptance of whole body training is utilized, to strengthen core muscle groups and add better muscle balance to the human organism. The 'newest and best work out of the week' approach is somewhat counterproductive and leads to confusion in the athlete, as to exactly what they should be doing to achieve their goals and at which part of their preparation should a particular type of run be emphasized. This book is focused and directed to long term training and is a solid program, using proven and technical information to achieve top potential and remove confusion in distance training. It works because it has been proven in the results of the best runners for decades. It has the newly added aspects of core strength to improve muscle balance and strength and lessen the incidence of injury. However, it is a system that needs to be followed segment by segment, without skipping ahead. The results an athlete receives are directly related to understanding these segments and why they are done in the order in which they are arranged. Training in this program also should include the use of light free weights, resistance machines and core exercises to balance the upper and lower body and the posterior and anterior body areas. The addition of core training and weight training used to be nearly unheard of for runners. But, we now train the entire system, while using the structured periods to maximize the ability of the athlete to train to race fitness, without injury. This is what makes this book unique and if a moderately trained runner begins to use this system, they should plan to adopt it long term. Many runners and the public in general today, tend to want results immediately. In this sport, 'achieving instant results' is not the mindset to adopt. The best of the best immerse themselves in the sport and use consistency and patience to achieve their highest potential. This is not to say they never have fun or lose all contact with daily life. But, the assigned workout is the focus when the running shoes are slipped on. The best athletes don't dread or overthink the day's workout. They already know what is scheduled and they take the first step out the door and do the work. Occasionally, the times are slower or the number of repetitions not achieved, but the workout itself is what the focus must be.

Consistency is incredibly important in achieving high level results. Originally, it was thought that working out three days a week was fine for fitness. This is certainly better than not at all, but there is not enough consistency in that type of fitness plan, to be of real use in increasing the fitness of any athlete. It can be of assistance to sedentary folks looking to slow deterioration of muscle strength and indeed, it has some benefits. But, we are not concerned with the normal, everyday maintenance of minimal cardiovascular fitness in this book. We are working here to build a better runner and then take that better runner to very high levels as an athlete. This is not easy, but you will be changed in body and mind forever, if you stick to it. So let's get with it.

PHASE ONE

BUILDING RUNNER ENDURANCE

The Distance Phase

The Distance Phase of this system is the single most important section of increasing fitness and strength in the runner and is the segment one must return to after reaching the 'peak' and racing for six to twelve weeks. Some runners have the notion they can 'race their way into shape'. This is counterproductive and is likely to result in overuse injuries, elevated lactic acid in the muscles and muscle tears, as the body as a whole, has not been base trained before racing at a peak level. Races can indeed be used as some of the runner's training, but not in the distance phase. For lactic acid rises too high too quickly and there are not enough mitochondria within the cells to make the runner effective and efficient. Racing hard during early training phases has other deleterious effects, as well. Lactic acid is a natural by-product of cell metabolism and it is more easily dealt with in trained muscles and is actually convert-ed back to an energy source component in the trained cell. Soreness is a sign of either the initial increase in mileage or going too fast too soon. The cell simply cannot return to nor-mal quickly if it is not trained to do so. So, what happens when we train? In this treatise, we will be concerned with cellular changes in relation to increasing the ability to use oxygen, the storage of and making use of fuel for long runs and increasing strength and speed for maximum performance during train-ing and racing. We will learn the relationship with the fuel stor-age tanks (mitochondria), oxygen availability and use during exercise and the methods to make a more efficient endurance machine. We do see track athletes work themselves to a peak by the late seasons, but they have absolutely done the base work before they increase the effort in their race schedules.

In order to increase mitochondria, VO2 uptake and the ability to focus for long racing, one must use a step system of increasing mileage, interspersed with regular rest periods, for several months at the onset of the first section of building endurance in the first year of serious training. For example, if one is running thirty miles per week or fifty miles at the outset of adopting this system, two things may be changed. The type of runs that are being performed each day and the rest between each, should be examined. If one is running too fast too often, peak performance will never be achieved. Lately, a system of pure interval training has come into the pop culture training circuit. This may give rapid strength increases for a time, but it is an incredible recipe for eventual breakdown and most of the runners who adopt this method of training, become injured, lose interest, or both. There simply, is no instant formula for fitness.

We will begin by running using a hard/easy weekly system. "Hard" in this phase, translates to distance, not speed. "Easy" is a lighter or shorter run or even a day off. No fast running will be done initially, but a mild 'tempo' run will be added several weeks into this Phase. Raising lactic acid too quickly is the recipe for injury or becoming a 'stale' performer. Below is an example of how an average hobby runner should get in thirty miles in the first week. Let's start with Sunday as day one and explain what the term 'easy' means in real time pace. This is a typical schedule for a normal, beginner runner, who can safely and comfortably run up to six miles as their long run.

Week one for the hobby runner- defined as one who is running thirty miles a week or less:

Sunday:

Run 6 miles easy. Easy is defined as a pace that will not raise the heartrate above 70% of maximum. To determine maximum heartrate, use the old formula of one's age, subtracted from 220. This is the average top heartrate of the low mileage hobby runner. For example, say one is 25 years old. The formula for running at 70% max, is calculated as essentially -(220) (-25) = 195 x.70 = 136.5.)

So, when you see 'easy', try to keep the heartrate approximately at the 60-70% level or as close as possible, with the necessary adjustments for age. There may be hills or occasional increases or decreases, but an average of 60-80% of maximum heartrate should keep the runner in an aerobic pace the body can handle without over stressing the cells to the point they cannot metabolize lactic acid efficiently.

Monday:

3 miles easy. Run 1st mile slow (below the 60% level of training effect), stretch lightly, then next two miles are run easy, but at the 70% level and stretch thoroughly again.

Tuesday:

5 easy. Repeat the Monday easy mile/stretch and easy 4 remaining miles and stretch again. Make sure all stretches are slow and are held to tension, not pain. (See stretching section).

Wednesday:
3 easy. Repeat Monday process. A light set of weights (see weight training section) should be included in this day after the run and then do the normal stretching routine.

Thursday:
6 easy. The warmup will be two miles slow, then stretch and complete the run and stretch again.

Friday:
3 easy. Repeat Monday process or if you are tired, take a rest day, but warmup and go through a set of very light weights and stretches, as in the Wednesday cycle.

Saturday:
This will be a tempo day. Yes, even in the Distance Phase, one will 'wake up' the fast twitch fiber with a mild faster section that will not raise lactic acid levels to a level that will be above normal, by the following day. 4 easy miles total for this workout. Warmup one mile, stretch and then run the next mile easy and the third mile, just a bit faster, but within the 75-80% aerobic percent VO2 maximum aerobic zone. The pace should be comfortable, aerobically, but should be 5-10% faster than the normal pace run during the week. This run will gradually move up in distance and pace, throughout the Distance Phase and will also be a part of most of the year round week's training. It aids in developing not only a greater ability to train faster, but

also helps the runner understand instinctively, his or her pace. The final mile should be comfortable. Stretch at completion.

The next and following weeks of this phase will increase in distance approximately 10% each week for two to three weeks and then level for one week and then up 10% again for two to three weeks and level out for one. This type of increase achieves the needed mileage gains, but allows the body to 'catch up' to the stress after each three week set of increases. Refer to the chart to understand how the increases should include the 'level off' weeks. The increases can be done a few different ways. First, each workout can have 10% added to its individual distance. Or, the athlete can select specific work-outs to increase, as long as the overall increase for the week is 10%. For instance, many runners will seek to increase the long run day, the tempo day and the mid distance day and let the 'easy' days stay low for longer. This is a good idea. However, as the overall mileage begins to gain serious momentum, there will certainly be a need to increase the distance in these light or easy days or even insert two workouts per day for the elite runner covering nearly one hundred miles per week.

FIRST YEAR- DISTANCE PHASE
I: INCREASE 10% **L:** LEVEL FROM PREVIOUS WEEK

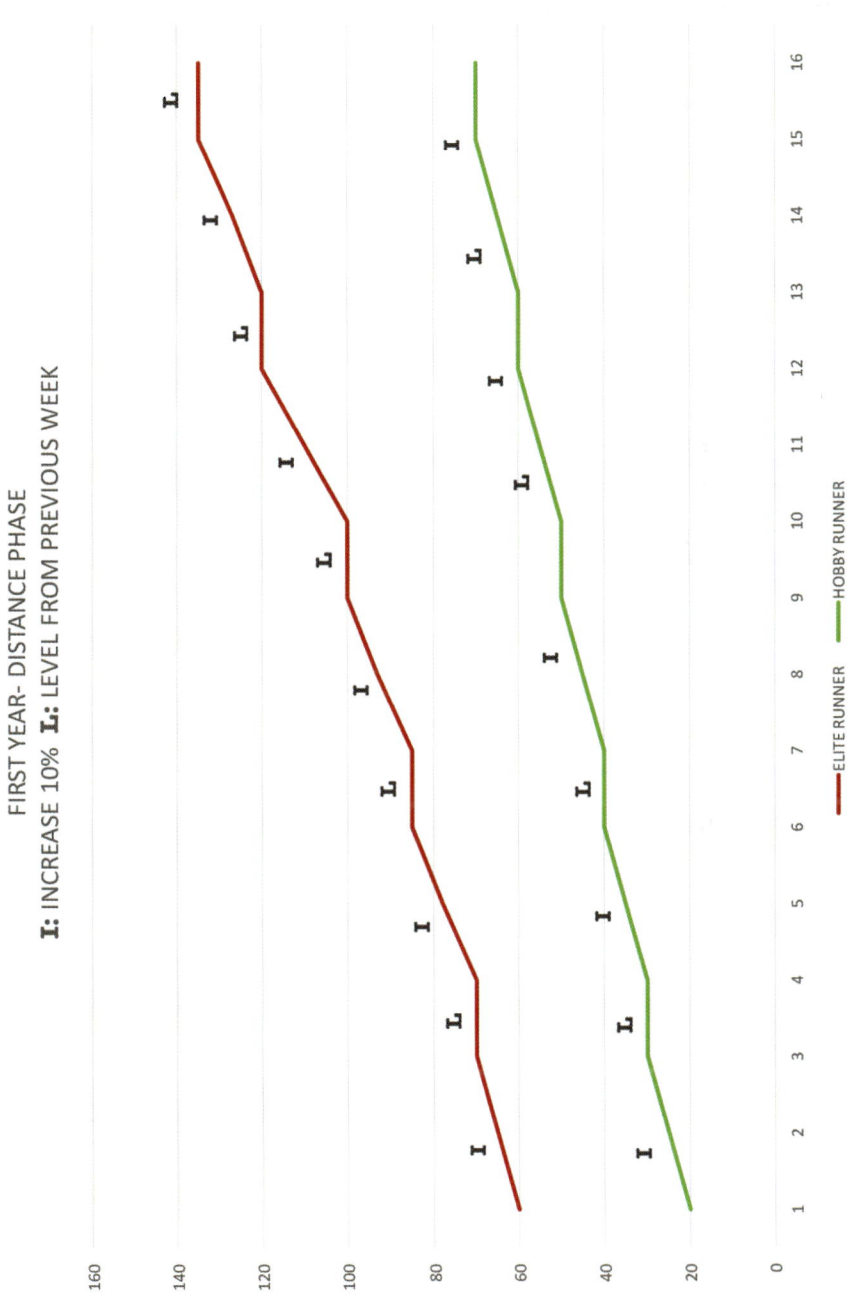

ELITE RUNNER HOBBY RUNNER

Note that mileage levels out every third week, then resumes 10% per week increase.

Tip: A reminder on when to stretch:
The human body will attempt to cool itself very quickly after any run, so make sure the main stretching routine is done quickly after the completion of the workout. Note, it is a good idea to stretch after the first mile or two warmup jog, as well. The muscles need to be heated before stretching, in order to lessen the chance of tearing. A mile or two of jogging will raise the muscle temperature to 102 degrees Fahrenheit. This is a good temperature to stretch a muscle, without triggering its protective inate tightening to prevent tears.

Waiting more than a few minutes is inviting the body to tighten up and lactic acid to rise higher. Stretch to tension, not pain. Stretching too hard can lead to small tears in muscle fiber, which can result in scar tissue within the muscle or ligaments. Focus on the hamstrings, the gastrocnemius group (the calf muscles), the lower back and the iliotibial band along the anterior area from the hip to the ankle. See the section on stretching to become more familiar with these stretches.

Weight Work Through the Phases

Weight resistance is now known to accomplish several helpful things for a runner, be they a sprinter or a marathoner. Begin using light weights and doing core work as you enter the initial Distance Phase. Three weight sessions a week is enough for a distance runner, as we are not seeking to build mass, but to create muscle balance. The key to using weights is to remember these simple rules:

- Use weights light enough to accomplish muscle fatigue or partial muscle failure at the end of 12-20 repetitions. Notice we don't attempt to achieve muscle failure sooner. We are indeed, working to build balanced strength along with endurance, so at times, the athlete will go up to 25 or more repetitions to utilize the endurance system in coordination with building strength.

- Three sets of each 'lift' should be used as a parameter, with a recovery time of no more than 60 seconds between sets.

- The idea, unless one is seeking to become a great sprinter from 100 to 200 meters, is to use the philosophy of 'low weight/high rep'. This prevents muscle bulk from increasing mass. A significant increase in mass in a distance runner will slow them down as it increases the amount of oxygen required to propel the runner and starts the use of the lactic acid system to move the runner forward for long distances. Distance runners want to keep lactic acid down for as long as possible. A sprinter, on the other hand, will benefit from higher weights and a bit more mass. The sprinter is using primarily, the lactic acid system, which does not use oxygen and is using fast twitch fiber, while only moving up to 200 meters at 100% effort. So, the sprinter, as opposed to the distance runner, will not only not be hindered by higher muscle mass, but will actually benefit from more thrust, provided from this setup.

Note that I do not have leg weight work included in this section. Leg extensions, reverse curls and toe raises can be helpful at times, but that work should be overseen by a qualified professional. The reason for this is flexion from horizontal, past the 30 degree 'bend', will begin to stretch the knee ligaments and tendons and the quadriceps and hamstrings, etc., will no longer be carrying the load of the weight. These exercises can be very helpful in knee rehabilitation, but should be directed by a physical therapist or qualified trainer. Besides, the Strength Phase will begin to add muscle to the quadriceps and the regular distance work tends to strengthen the anterior muscles through most of the Phases.

Runner Beneficial Weight Work

- Military Press
- Standing Curls
- Flys
- Bench Press

Do not forget to work the abdominals, through crunches and/ or crunches with light weight held against the chest.

Now we have achieved a thirty mile week, using a hard/easy system. This is an example of the workout week of someone who has started running a few months or even a year prior, but now wants to find their true potential. This schedule is going to take you there. The 'hard' refers to longer versus shorter distances, in this phase, not faster versus slower. This terminology will change somewhat, as the runner moves from one section of training to the next. The following weeks should see increased mileage, using very gradually increasing aerobic pace, at about 10% for the week. Every two to three weeks of increases in mileage will be followed by a level off for the following week and then a resumption of the 10% increase. During this phase, two of the days will take the brunt of the increases in mileage. For instance, if you choose Sunday as your long day, it will go to 7 miles and Thursday will add one more mile, as well. Two of the easy days will add only ½ mile each or you may add one mile to one of the mid-level tempo runs. After three weeks of this type of increase and your 'level' week, you will shift more mileage to your "long" day and a bit less of the increase to your midweek run. You will be surprised at how soon the mileage has increased. In fact, after the first six to eight weeks, this increase becomes exponential. Use care, however. Speed is a bad word during this initial phase, especially if you have been used to going fast one or two days a week. Let the desire for very fast running go until you get to fifty miles a week. The tempo runs, as noted, are fairly quick, but are still in the aerobic range and will not initiate the lactic acid system. And the Distance Phase section of training is the longest. Why? If you paid attention in the early explanation of how the cell changes, you will accept the fact that the body is changing and you must be a bit patient. When you get to fifty miles per week, you will be strong enough to pick up the pace naturally and all of your days are longer in distance. Besides, as fitness increases, your 60-80% level will allow a faster pace, due to higher strength, lower resting heartrate and gained endurance. A good way of monitoring the correct speed you should be running, is to continue monitoring your heartrate. Watch how the resting rate drops and how you are able to run a faster pace without achieving your 80% maximum heart-rate level. Week after week, the heart and vascular system improves and the amount of blood pumped with each stroke increases, so the number of beats needed to achieve oxygen saturation, decreases. This occurs throughout the body, as it will begin to add more capillaries, increase the size of the left ventricle (the main pumping chamber of oxygenated blood), increase the arterial and venous sizes and the runner will usually develop a more efficient form, as they pile up the miles. See the section on form, to understand how important this is to the speed and efficiency of a runner.

The first year of training, the Distance Phase lasts for up to sixteen weeks. In subsequent years, this Phase will be shorter, as the athlete is already running higher mileage on a steady basis. After one develops a weekly long run of twenty miles, a midweek run of fifteen miles and the total mileage is 80-100 miles for the week for a now high level athlete, the runner will be able to level off. Those who wish to run less total miles will still be in condition to go through their Phases more quickly. There may be a need to do two workouts a day on some days, in order to get the mileage in for the elite runner. As long as the runner has become more experienced, it is ok to go up to 100+ miles a week for the last few weeks of the Distance Phase. Use extreme caution in building mileage during this phase. Pay attention to small pains and fatigue. Rest is extremely important between workouts now, so the more time off your feet you can achieve, the better. Use stretching when the muscles are warm. Never try to stretch a cold muscle, as noted in the first week of the low mileage Distance Phase example. A warm muscle is from 102 degrees to 103 degrees. It is best done after very slow jogging for 5-10 minutes or even right after a hot shower or steam/sauna if there will be a necessity to delay stretching right after the workout. Too many runners walk out the door and start stretching, then go right into a workout, thinking they are now loose. Wrong. Stretch after a slow jog in the first mile or two. The muscle temperatures should be high enough at this point to do a gentle set of stretching, focusing on the hamstrings and the anterior and posterior lower leg muscles. Use the section on stretching to give a basic guide of the muscles to focus on for certain workouts and general lengthening of the muscles most likely to be affected during any particular workout. Then, do another thorough set of stretches after the run. As the runner gets to the end of the sixteen week Distance Phase and has achieved a fairly high mileage weekly schedule, the weekly workout sessions may look something like this:

Sunday:
20-22 miles easy

Monday:
8 miles easy with a weight workout at the end and stretching.

Tuesday:
10 miles easy

Wednesday:
run 16 miles, with the five middle miles of the workout at tempo pace* (again, see the definition of 'tempo' below) and a weight workout at the end of the session, just before the stretching process. Remember, if the weight workout cannot be done immediately, while the muscle is warm, stretch and then do the weight session as soon as possible. Always start

the weight session with very light weights, some stretching of the upper body and then the main body of the workout.

Thursday:
Jog 5 miles in the a.m. and run 10 miles in the p.m. easy, but at a solid pace. Stretch slowly and thoroughly, concentrating on the hamstring groups, the calves or gastrocnemius muscles, the quadriceps and the core.

Friday:
13 miles at an easy pace. Stretching and/or yoga should wrap up the workout, as usual.

Saturday:
Jog 6 miles easy in the a.m. and run 10 miles easy in the p.m. Do a light weight workout after the second run and perform your stretching and/or yoga. Even though focusing on stretching the running muscle groups as your main concern is important, good overallflexibility is always a good thing. See the stretching section for help in this area.

This is a 90 mile week. Notice, however, that the Distance Phase graph for the Hobby Runner shows about 60-65 miles a week at the end of the Distance Phase. This paragraph assumes you will have a bit more experience at the beginning of your section and therefore, you have achieved a bit higher mileage at the end of the sixteen weeks. If you haven't, do not feel you have underachieved. We will all have goals that differ slightly. The point is to follow the schedule and build endurance during the four months of mileage building, during year one. Additionally, note that there is a leveling off every two to three weeks in the Distance Phase. We are letting the body catch up to the higher mileage and more time on the road. And notice now that a faster tempo* run is allowed. A runner at this level can handle the gentle beginning of faster workouts, even before reaching the second section of this program. In fact, each section gradually merges with the next, as the section gets within three weeks of the upcoming one. Better experienced runners will be able to add mileage to this schedule to achieve 100 or more miles for the week. The runner will stay at this Distance Building Phase for sixteen weeks and retain the 80-100 mile week level for the last three to four weeks, before moving to the next phase. In case you are still confused as to determining your tempo pace, here is a more detailed explanation. *Tempo pace is the speed one would run a typical 5k race, but at about only 85% of that race pace. For example, if you are able to race a 15-16 minute 5k at this point, tempo pace would be at a 17:30 minute 5k pace. Two workouts maximum per week may be at tempo pace for the more highly trained and experienced runner, but only 10% of the total week's mileage should be at the above described tempo pace. This addition to the slower distance pace keeps a bit of spark in the legs, but does not build high levels of lactic acid before the muscles are ready to metabolize it. By the time a runner is covering 80-100 miles per week, the tempo section can be up to fourteen miles in two 7 mile sections in length on two of the athlete's days. If the high level runner is doing only one tempo session a week, that distance may be 10 miles in the middle of a fifteen mile workout.

Again, for the hobby runner, the highest weekly mileage achieved may only be fifty miles a week, but a goal is a goal.

During this building phase, the muscle cell is changing to adapt to higher levels of stress and is chemically more efficient under that stress. Lactic acid levels stay lower for longer periods and there have been more mitochondria created in the cell to handle and store more glycogen for use as fuel. The cell can liberate this glycogen in the presence of more supplied oxygen, in the process called glycolysis. Note glycolysis is the main pathway for the production of heat generated from the production of adenosine triphosphate, in the presence of, but not dependent on O2. So, why are we working so hard to increase the ability of the body to assimilate and use more oxygen, through long runs? Notice I said 'in the presence of' O2. Without oxygen present in this chemical reaction, waste products of CO_2 and water cannot be expelled and the cell reaction will shut down. This is why sprinters have to stop running at 100% effort in a fairly short distance. Lactic acid has built up in their fast twitch fibers and they are running essentially, without oxygen as a part of their sprint. That is the lactic acid process we discussed regarding short fast bursts. Runners who utilize this book and already are able to run about fifty miles a week comfortably, will reach the 100-120 mile level more quickly, though they should also never increase overall weekly mileage by more than 10% per week. This will be stressed over and over here, as increases in mileage at too high a rate, exhaust the muscle stores, fatigue the muscle and lead to injury. Those who start at about 20-30 miles per week and wish to be better Hobby Runners will achieve about 60-70 miles at the end of the Distance Phase. And that is proper for the first building year. Besides the tempo runs, overall pace will naturally increase, as more alveoli are developed and muscle memory improves, as a reaction to the expectation of the stress of regular, consistent workouts. They will just have the advantage of being able to do their distance phase at a bit quicker overall pace, due to a good baseline of fitness from the first week. But, they are also required to use proper rest in between workouts and rest becomes more and more important throughout the entire program. Some world class runners sleep twelve hours a night. This may not be practical for 'normal folks' who go to work every day, but sleep is only part of rest. Relaxation and 'decompressing', using things like yoga or other meditative techniques can be of great help to the working athlete and can even be practiced at work, many times.

NOTE:

Rest in between each hard workout has another beneficial effect, besides just the physical rebuilding of cells and increasing strength. Psychologically, the continuous stress of physically pushing a body that is not properly equipped for high intensity exercise can psychologically tire the athlete and lead to 'staleness' in performance or even injury to muscle and ligament groups that have not been trained to retain good form and foot plant during training or racing. Focus can only be achieved for a limited amount of time. The mind must be rested, as well as the body in between exercise sessions. We can see the deterioration in focus in all athletes as the event lengthens, when the runner has not trained the brain, as well as the muscle. I once, as just an offhand question, asked a training partner how he found the resilience to lace his shoes twice a day and do the workout. He remarked "I purposely do not think about it". Just his mulling it over before the prescribed workout caused a mental state of dread or anxiety at times. So, to race too often or train too many miles too quickly before properly strengthening the body and mental focus , can be catastrophic. And over thinking the prescribed workout can literally talk the runner out of a good session. Deep sleep helps this recovery and taking the mind off the sport at times, is wise. This is yet another reason the hard/easy system is used. Psychological balance leads to better physical performance. Over racing or over training are equally destructive. Recently, in our 'instant results' mindset developed in the last several years, there has been a movement to go straight to interval and weight training, while bypassing the base of aerobic training. This may give temporarily better strength and race times, but there is literally, trouble down the road. Few athletes or even casual racers succeed for very long with this type of training regimen. One of the reasons the Europeans and Africans are able to perform well and have long careers, is that they are not inundated with the "workout of the week guaranteed to be the answer" advertising and publications we see nowadays. Some may feel the system at times may be boring, dated or not produce results quickly enough, but it is unethical to recommend a training system for just today. Additionally, the best race only when ready to race and use patience to their advantage. Besides, after over fifty years associated with the sport and studying most of the workouts designed to produce results too quickly, this author is certain this system works. Most athletes, not just elites, want to stay in their sport long term. The very best have been patient and analytical in their training, thus limiting their chance of injury and being able to plan their race season accurately and with consistently better results.

Words of Wisdom:

I had a 1,500 meter world record holder tell me how it was fairly easy to beat the Americans most of the time, because we, as a society, are too focused on racing without being prepared. He remarked how he took a full month off every year and just relaxed and played informal soccer with friends. His times were proof of the power of focus, rest and a properly structured training system. The best know when to rest.

Training at Altitude

One of the advantages the African elite runners have, that has now also begun to be used by our own Olympic coaching system, is the natural aid of training at altitude. When a runner trains at altitudes of 1500 to 2,000 meters, essentially the 5,000 to 7,000 foot elevation of the mountains of Kenya and other East African countries, the body begins to adapt to the added stress of less available oxygen to run the body's systems. Hemoglobin levels rise, red cells increase, myoglobin increases and the lungs adapt. However, these adaptations should be not taken for granted. The speed at which the athlete trains should be reduced initially, when going to altitude and gradually increased as the body begins the bio-physical changes occurring from elevation training. There is another aspect of this training to consider. When should the sea level athlete seek to take advantage of this boost and how long will it last? Normally, most high level runners will go to elevation for four to six weeks during the Strength Phase and through the initial ten days of the Speed Phase. Those ath-letes who live full time at altitude will not wrestle with this issue. It takes about ten days after returning to sea level for the systems to mature and the effects can last another four to eight weeks. If you are a serious runner and you have the support to try it, why not? The Kenyans are not just natural runners because of mass to body ratio. They have this now, not so secret, tool in their training to take advantage of. Plus, these athletes grow up in these mountainous regions and are adapted from birth, to thrive at higher altitudes. Our Olympic Training Center moved to altitude in Colorado to take advan-tage of this. It is proven to assist and give the athlete that little edge they may need.

For runners who already live at higher elevations, like Denver or the Eastern Blue Ridge or other mountainous ar-eas, you will still follow this same schedule as people living at sea level. You will just have this 'built in' advantage to your training. The next section, called the Strength Phase that in-cludes hard charging uphill and some faster downhill running, will still be followed, as well, but you will want to increase the number of repetitions and run hard enough to raise your heartrate to recommended stress levels to stimulate the increase in alveoli, hemoglobin, myoglobin and 'heme'. Both sea level and altitude living runners have a terrific increase and advantage from simulation or actual running at altitude. I say 'simulation' here, because there are products and masks on the market that actually reduce the oxygen one is getting, thus letting the body know it has to change in order to survive this stress. They are not, to my knowledge harmful, as the body will naturally have to slow to be able to proceed. As the body becomes adjusted to altitude, it will be in an essentially legal super body state. One thing that will never be recommended in this treatise is the use of illegal steroids or even HGH. HGH is human growth hormone. Some athletes have used steroids and HGH to have an advantage in competition, particularly the Olympics. Testing that shows the presence of these and other illegal drugs, means immediate disqualification and if a medal has been won, it will be stripped from the athlete, as it should.

This is why we use things like the natural adaptations of altitude and good, planned training to be an athlete. The altitude advantage provided when coming down to sea level running, lasts from four to six weeks, as the body will dissipate and eliminate the extra 'heme' and higher hemoglobin levels after that time. Besides, 'free heme' by itself, is not a great asset to the body. When actual hemoglobin is circulated, each hemoglobin molecule can bind four molecules of oxygen, thus increasing the ability to disperse oxygen to cells. One downside of this higher amount of platelets and red cells in the blood stream is the higher viscosity of the flow stream. Anyone who has not been properly vetted for heart disease in the family should use caution here. As was noted at the beginning of this book, running and even elite runner status, will improve heart health dramatically, but will not make an athlete immune from disease and death. Train properly, as recommended here, but include your physician in your plan. In fact, choose a physician who is skilled in sports and sports medicine. Runner athletes are different than what most physicians see. Most physicians see people who may have disease resulting from obesity, smoking, over drinking or a sedentary lifestyle. That isn't us. Make sure your doctor understands the body of an athlete.

But I Only Run 5k's and 10k races!

Now, the miler, 5,000 meter, 10,000 meter and marathon runner will all use the first Phase to build endurance and ability to perform. Their specific training schedules are addressed in later chapters. During this first Phase, all are concerned with increasing the ability of the lungs and the alveoli of same, to take up oxygen from respiration and excrete carbon dioxide and water on the exhale. The difference in training for these races is the ratio and intensity of the strength and speed work to slow distance runs. And that occurs only after the base has been established. If a runner has established a solid base, they will be able to race occasionally, but it is recommended the runner use races during this time sparingly and not at an all-out pace. These are training runs, designed to prepare the athlete for developing the tactic of racing, not the speed.

Additionally, there is a bit of natural selection that will determine which distance the athlete should focus upon. The marathoner tends to have a high ratio of slow twitch fiber to fast twitch fiber. Slow twitch fiber uses more glycogen and oxygen for most of the energy produced, whereas fast twitch fiber uses the anaerobic or lactic acid cycle for the shorter, faster movement and duration of the event, as mentioned earlier. After a year on this program, one will understand the distance they are best suited to concentrate on and the area they will have the best chance of high level success. These races and the training for each will be discussed in a later section.

Training in Heat
NEGATIVES AND POSITIVES (SEE INJURIES, AS WELL)

At this point, it is very relevant to discuss the adjustments one must make while training in heat, as the runner is piling up the miles and dehydration and heat stress becomes an issue to carefully monitor. Training unwisely in heat, can kill. The Distance Building Phase is the longest phase of the program for a reason. There are major changes the body undergoes during this section and it is best to have them occur on a consistent, but relatively cautious schedule. The muscle cells are increasing mitochondria, the lungs are developing more alveoli and the hypothalamus is adapting to the stress of higher temperatures within the body. The proper function of the hypothalamus is critical to internal temperature regulation, particularly during summer training. The runner will need to train nearly year round in order to retain muscle memory, though summer training differs from fall and winter training. In warm climates, summer temperatures and high humidity can be lethal to an untrained runner and can kill even a trained runner that does not properly plan, prepare and pace. The summer is for slow training and building. The environment actually allows the runner to go slower during the hot summer and still stress the body to make the changes we want to see in the Building Phase. A good tip to use when training in humidity over 60% and ambient air temperatures of 75-80 degrees Fahrenheit or higher, is to note body weight before and after the workout. A loss of 3% of body weight at the end of a workout means hydration is inadequate. Get in the habit of weighing yourself before and after each session and recording this. In parallel, heartrate will be higher, even at slower speeds, as we struggle to cool our core, so training effect actually occurs even at these slower speeds. We cool our bodies by producing sweat and the evaporation of same. Exhaling air also removes heat, though sweat is more efficient. The added stress of heat allows us to reduce speed and still stress the body enough to stimulate training effect. By ensuring the athlete is drinking enough cool fluid, the training can go longer and most of all, safer. But, if the weather is hot, the runner will always be in a deficit of fluid intake to outflow. So, learn to drink even when you are not thirsty and learn to drink on the run or during the workout. The body absorbs fluids faster if the fluid is at approximately 45 degrees Fahrenheit. Another factor to consider along with fluid intake is the question of what type of fluid to drink. Many studies have been done on the correct ratio of glucose and electrolytes in fluids that may enhance absorption, performance and indeed, survival. The first and foremost, is water. Water is the fluid to concentrate on. In long runs and long races, each individual will have to experiment with the type of fluid to take in during the training or racing period. Heavily sugared and/or salted fluid is difficult for the stomach to absorb. As I trained in hot weather year round, water was my fluid of choice. If I used a commercial fluid replacement drink at all, I usually cut it by half with pure water, as my stomach did not accept sweet drinks during a run very well. Glucose containing drinks are indeed important for recovery and slightly sweetened drinks with electrolytes are helpful in longer races and for more rapid recovery. If an athlete is taking in a proper amount of nutrition, additional electrolytes will usually not be needed. However, potassium, magnesium, sodium, calcium and chloride need to be in homeostasis within the cell. Potassium and magnesium seem to be the two electrolytes most often pointed to, as problems occur. Make sure the diet includes plenty of foods that include these. We have more sodium chloride in our diets than we need already, so use "runner" foods for heat, like melon, tomatoes and other fruits, to supplement your diet. A severe deficiency of these balanced electrolytes and water can disrupt electrical signals in the heart and irregular heartbeat can occur and even kill, if not addressed. Also, the replacement of glycogen stores quickly after a workout will make recovery occur faster and more efficiently. Make sure you read your body. A physician can run tests to determine if chronic deficiencies of electro-lytes or hemoglobin are affecting health. Practice with the drinks you plan to take in during races. Use them, on the run if you are able, but stopping briefly to replenish fluids will usu-ally help, not hurt, overall time. Bill Rodgers found it difficult to 'drink on the run', so he would come to a complete stop to drink water during marathons. This distressed onlookers and his coaches, but it was Bill's way and it worked well for him. So, practice taking in fluids during your hard training runs and you will find out what is right for you.

REVIEW OF PHASE ONE

THE DISTANCE PHASE

Now, to review the distance phase of year one, the runner must establish a starting mileage, run a hard/easy schedule, keep the training heartrate between 60-80% of maximum heartrate function and build for at least sixteen weeks to achieve proper baseload levels and strength to move into the second section of training. Several factors are to be monitored: resting heartrate, hydration, sleep, caloric intake and weight, increasing distance by no more than 10% per week, balancing and strengthening core group muscles like the abdominals and using care to address small pains before they become chronic injury. It is very important, as mileage increases, to keep the abdomen and other 'front facing' muscles strong, as running tends to over strengthen and shorten the lower back muscles, hamstrings and gluteal muscles. See the supplementary and complimentary exercises that will be helpful, in the chapter dedicated to strength and stretching exercises. These exercises will be a part of normal training through most of the week, from week one to the day before the race. Think of the body as a fine sports car. There are a myriad of things that must be maintained, but when maintenance is consistent, the machine runs well.

Plateau Your Schedule

As the runner increases mileage, it is very important to level off mileage approximately every two to three weeks, for two consecutive weeks. (See graph, page 91). This allows the body to 'catch up' in strength and fitness before moving into higher mileage. Practicing this philosophy will help to reduce the incidence of overuse injury due to muscle fatigue. This may seem like a small point, but it can make the difference between continuing on schedule and taking an enforced rest due to injury and soreness. Don't be as rigid as to incur an injury during this phase, but do strive for strong consistency. In fact, if I had to pick between harder workouts with less workout days and slightly less intense workouts, but on a more consistent basis, I would choose the latter. Rest does not mean sacrificing consistency. One can cross train with swimming or even walking during the rest days if necessary. Muscle memory is developed through consistent training over long periods of time.

The more highly developed high school or college level runner can stay consistent and run six to seven days a week, where the Hobby Runner who has just decided to really go after higher goals, may have the ability to run only five days a week and walk or swim the other two. But, they are still moving and the body recognizes that. Besides, their overall mileage is still increasing, be it for the Hobby or the Elite runner, throughout the Distance Phase.

As the Distance Phase is gradually coming to an end, strength is growing and has become a normal part of the daily workout. In fact, the Second Phase, the Strength Phase, is gradually becoming merged into the Distance Phase, before it is officially incorporated as its own Phase. The runner has become more fit and will find themselves running their daily sessions at a faster pace than week one. Their tempo runs will be easier, but use a bit of caution not to fall into the trap of turning the workout into a race. This is very easy to do when running with a group, so run with athletes who are at or a bit better than your level. An athlete who is much more advanced will end up hurting you, though not intentionally. It is just their level, not yours.

The Distance Phase will start to lightly mimic the next Phase by the time the athlete has gotten to week twelve. However, the next Phase will have some very different aspects that will be added to the distance one is covering. There will be differences in muscle groups used and the sessions will adapt the body to the strength needed to utilize speed and run hills, among other things.

CHAPTER TWO

THE RESISTANCE PHASE
(STRENGTH RESISTANCE)

Why would one seek to build endurance before strength? The two actually go hand in hand. Distance training, in addition to building endurance, prepares the body to 'shift gears' to harder workouts, designed to increase the ability of the body to push uphill and hold pace at longer distances. Adding in the resistance of gravity, such as hill running, alerts the muscles to adapt to this new stressor.

The distance the athlete is now running will be modified, but not reduced. We will now add resistance to the weekly sessions to increase strength in the quadriceps, which tend to receive less increase in strength compared to the anterior groups during the distance phase, plus upper body strength for power during hard hill racing and 'end of race push' ability. We will now begin to add hill sessions, or if the runner has no hills to use, treadmills set at angles from 2% to 8% for intervals of one minute each to seven minutes each. The speed the runner will be training at during these uphill sections will be the same or as close to normal distance run training pace, as possible. Naturally, Elite runners will have a much faster normal training pace than the Hobby runners.

The approach will resemble the technique used in the distance phase, but with an important difference built in. The athlete will use three of the weekly workouts to build adaptation through resistance, at an increasing workload, while still running a hard/easy schedule. The reason for adding the strength and resistance work after the distance build up, is to 'wake up' additional types and areas of muscle cells and add strength to our endurance. Some use of the terms 'strength' and 'endurance' will be used interchangeably, but generally we can think of endurance as utilizing slow twitch fiber and oxygen for covering ground and strength will utilize a combination of slow and fast twitch fiber. So far, we have primarily focused on the slow twitch fiber cell and building oxygen carrying systems. The mitochondria, or energy factories, are fully capable of carrying the runner twenty miles using primarily glycogen, but adding in the metabolism of fat for part of the early miles and more of the later miles. One of the reasons a runner slows down in the latter stages of a marathon, is the necessity to begin burning fat, as glycogen stores are depleted. In the Distance Phase, we focused on running long at least twice a week. There was a method to that madness. When an endurance athlete is in the early stages of a long event, they have the use of primarily glycogen as fuel. Glycogen can release 4kcal per liter of oxygen, yet fat needs 9kcal/liter. Fat is dense and is more difficult for the cell to utilize as fuel. With repetitive long runs, the body begins to absorb and metabo-lize glycogen and fat more efficiently, as higher amounts of O2 are now able to be absorbed and energy is available from both. The lungs have developed more alveoli to take up oxygen and the transport systems to the muscles are now highly developed. That, in simple terms, means the athlete will be equipped to burn fat more efficiently in the late stages of a marathon or other race of 20 miles or more without slowing as much. The body stores about 1,800 calories in the form of glycogen. Approximately 1,500 are stored in the muscles and another 300-500 can be stored in the liver. If a runner is using the standard of burning approximately 100 or so calories per mile for a 150 pound person, at about the 18-20 mile mark there will have to be a shift in the ratio and types of fuel used. Practicing running long has begun to adapt the body to make the shift from burning glycogen to burning fat easier. This strength section is helpful in making all muscle cells more efficient.

- Think of the use of fuel in the body as the way a race car would use energy. Consider the incredibly high powered drag race automobiles. Nitro funny cars burn nitroglycerin based fuels, as they burn hot and fast. Stock race cars have much further to go, so using a fuel that will hold a pretty high efficiency of burning, without overheating the machine, is preferable for a distance runner.

So, how does the Strength Phase section differ from our Distance Phase buildup? We will now use the advantage of 'gravity multiplied', to increase and diversify our cell system efficiency. Here is an example of the first resistance phase week:

Week One of Resistance/Strength Example:

Sunday:
20-22 miles easy (note 'easy' will be faster now that the athlete has trained consistently for the last four months to achieve a good, solid base, higher hemoglobin to transport the oxygen and more mitochondria to burn said oxygen).

Monday:
Run an easy 8 miles on flat surface. Light upper body curls, presses, flys core crunches are also done on these days. Use a weight that will require 20-25 repetitions to achieve muscle failure.

Tuesday:
Warmup 2 miles easy, stretch and then begin repeat hill work. High speed is not the factor here. The pure resistance of the hill will produce the strength to begin increasing speed. Run two minutes at a 3% incline at low stress aerobic pace. If one is now properly trained, 'easy' may be as fast as 6-7 minutes per mile. You will know if you are in distress and use heartrate for

the early weeks of resistance if that is easier for you to gauge low stress, but brisk pace. If you use heartrate for you gauge, you will be hitting between 80-90% of your VO2 max after the third hill. Like every workout, you should increase pace and resistance as the workout goes from beginning until the cool down. This will essentially teach your body to run races with a negative split mentality. Remember, every record you will ever see, is run with negative splits. Look at the mile run on TV. The first 800 will sometimes have a 'rabbit' to take the group through the first half, so there will be no lagging. The third lap will see a significant acceleration and the last lap will be a full on race, with a highly trained miler able to run the last 250 meters at top speed in a complete anaerobic state. Tunnel vision sets in about 200 meters from the finish and the last 100 is a literal blur and blacking out while on their feet is not uncommon. We aren't asking you to do this in a workout, but you are tuning your body to handle anything thrown at it, with the next Phase making you into the best runner you NEVER believed you could be. Recover by jogging at a level angle for one minute. Then, set the angle to 4%. Run easy at that angle for two minutes. Then, return to level (1.5% on a treadmill) for one and a half minutes. Go up to 4% for three minutes at an easy pace. Then back down to level for two minutes. Go back up to 3% for two minutes. Then finish the workout (12 total miles) at level ground and an easy pace. Please note this tip, when using a treadmill instead of a hill to provide the workout. Do not lower the angle of the treadmill to 0% for 'normal' miles. Raise it to 1.5% angle. The reason for this is quite simple. At fully level, the belt is passing beneath your feet, rather than you pushing across the ground. So, by increasing the angle slightly, the actual push across level ground is better mimicked. Stretch and work the core on this day, as well.

Wednesday:
Easy 3 miles in the a.m. and an easy 5 miles in the p.m. Make sure you are stretching warm muscles during all of this phase, as the resistance you are utilizing will tighten the anterior and posterior muscle groups. 8 miles total. Run this on a flat surface.

Thursday:
Warmup 2 miles. Start the resistance with two minutes at 3%, then move down to level for one minute at an easy pace. Raise the level to 4% for three minutes. Then go down to level for one and a half minutes. Then up to 5% for three minutes at an easy pace. Then, move down to level for two minutes. Then, up to 3% for three minutes. Finish the rest of the workout at a 1.5% angle and get 12 miles total in for the workout. Always remember the core. Weights are used again this day.

Friday:
Easy 4 miles in the a.m. and easy 6 miles in the p.m. 10 miles total. This is run on a flat surface. Stretch and work the core abdominals, as usual.

Saturday:
Warmup of 3 miles. Then up to 3% for three minutes. Move down to level for two minutes. Raise the level up to 3% for four minutes and down to level for four minutes. Move up to 4% for three minutes and down to level for the rest of the workout. Total mileage for this workout should be 12 miles. Stretch and rest well after this workout. Remember, your long day is coming again tomorrow.

Note the total mileage for the week is 84. A highly trained runner should add one more uphill to each of the three resistance days and add from 6-10 more level miles total for the first resistance week. By the third week, the mileage will be at about 90 for the base trained (runner who started with 50 miles a week at the beginning of the distance phase), and back to 100+ miles for the highly trained runner. The 'hill' will also go up. After three weeks of the resistance phase, the hill should be raised by one percent for each of the inclines. By week six, the hill should be as follows: 4, 5, 6, 6, 7, 7% for the incline series and for those living in hilly areas, the athlete will just spend more time on the hills and the speed should increase to 85-90% of Max VO2 on the uphills. Total time in resistance mode during the eight weeks of the section will be approximately 20% of the workout at week one and 50% at week eight. This is important to remember, as we are not just maintaining higher overall mileage in this phase, but we are now adding in increasing strength and resistance each week. Also, note to recover enough between sets to bring the heartrate down to the 60% Max. The final miles of each workout of this section will be at least two miles, but up to four if necessary to achieve the week's mileage. Stretching right after the run is very important during a resistance phase. The anterior muscle and ligament groups of the legs have been stressed, but now so have the posterior groups. So, both areas will require slow, but consistent stretches, in order to keep the natural order of muscle shortening as strength increases, from occurring. Plus, a longer muscle can contract further and faster when trained, resulting in greater speed.

One issue with using a treadmill for all hill training, is the problem of never going downhill. Downhill running must be practiced, if the athlete is to understand the effects of gravity on the quadriceps and ankles. Try to find a normal hill to use, at least part of the time one is doing resistance work. If one has a bridge with a safe running path across it, that type of hill will suffice. Athletes sometimes believe they can make up time on downhills and this is somewhat true, but downhills are very hard on the quadriceps, so the smart athlete practices this part of hill racing. Run downhills in races fast, but not out of control. You will pay if you do. See the comments on stress fractures in the injury section of this book.

Some soreness is to be expected during the initial phase of this section. However, runners who normally train in some hilly country should be able to ease into this phase without soreness and additionally, hill country trained runners should increase each of these angles by 1% at the outset of the second phase and add two more repetitions to all hill days This is important due to the fact the hill trained runner may find the initial phase of this section to be a bit too easy.

Remember the basics. This cannot be stressed too often.. Hydration, proper nutrition, rest and using a hard/easy schedule and staying flexible all apply in each phase. Let the resistance take care of itself. At week three, begin to increase the first hill by 1%, the second hill by the same and the last two by 1.5%. By week six, the runner should be doing six to eight hills during the resistance days and should continue this schedule through the rest of the strength/resistance phase. If the runner lives and runs in a hilly area, just substitute by using the hills you have. You cannot change the hill, but you can change the attack of the hill.

The runner will be tempted to attack the hills as he or she gains more fitness. This is ok, but 'attack' means just running a tempo pace on the uphill sections (85% of max VO2). Max is defined as the fastest pace a runner can hold without incurring oxygen debt. Attacking the hills too hard during this phase will raise lactic acid levels too high. The hill work itself will begin the process of the cell adapting to the metabolism of lactic acid and more efficient processing of oxygen and elimination of CO_2 through more alveoli in the lungs. Let the body adapt. This process cannot be rushed, if the runner wants to become faster and retain fitness longer. Yet another factor to consider in hill and every other type of training is the density of the training surface. Concrete has a higher density than asphalt and asphalt is higher in density than a grass or dirt surface. So, consider this when deciding where to do your training runs.

This is an interesting phase. The runner will literally see the body change. Additional muscle definition will appear and upper body muscular mass may increase. The reason for this is simple. The runner has now introduced a different muscle cell type into the mix. The fast twitch fiber is now being utilized, even though the runner is not actually running fast. The fast twitch cell is the 'power' cell and fires off quickly to help the athlete get uphill without going into complete oxygen deficit. The fast twitch cell is technically not an aerobic functioning cell, but it is available now to aid the runner during this stress phase. We want to bring this cell along gradually, just as the slow twitch cell. Too much lactic acid production at the onset of this phase results in breakdown. We will be in this phase for eight weeks, so there is no need to rush this process. At the end of this section, the runner will be both extremely aerobically fit and now able to call on the fast twitch cell for the beginning of the speed work phase.

Weights and the Runner:
Strength through Speed Phase:

During this segment, it is helpful to begin using light free weights to strengthen shoulder and arm muscles for 'pushing' during tough parts of races and increasing ability to retain good form. We have been using weights mildly from day one, but now the athlete will increase the weight by 5-10% and go to a three session per week schedule. Good form increases kinetic efficiency and helps the runner actually use less effort to run faster. Heavy weights (defined here as the amount of weight a person can only do 8-10 repetitions of, without muscle failure), are not necessary or even recommended for distance runners focusing on 1,500 meters and above. Every weight workout should be low weight/high repetition, but the athlete is now able to use the slightly higher weight and still get the high repetitions in. The amount of weight used for curls, military press, 'flys' or bench pulls can be experimented with to see the number of repetitions one can handle. Females may want to use as low as 5-10 pounds, for the first few sessions and move up if the weight is too easy to lift. The same principles apply to males, as well. Males will usually have more pure weight lifting strength, so they may start with heavier weights, but the point is to build strength without increasing body mass significantly. Heavy runners have to move more weight, using higher strength and fighting the force of gravity. Body size and mass relates pretty closely to the sport the athlete excels at. I have never seen a 125 lb. Kenyan marathoner excel as an offensive lineman in the NFL. Neither have I seen a 300 lb. lineman run a sub - 2:10 marathon. This may sound trite, but remember you are molding your body to the sport, not the other way around.

The same 10% principle of increasing resistance each week, applies to the strength phase. The distance buildup phase used this to get to the high level of endurance the athlete needed to shift to the strength phase. Now, the 10% rule continues to apply in the strength phase. The Resistance Phase consists of changes to two to three workouts per seven day exercise week.

A typical strength session will consist of a two mile warmup, then uphill running at an incline from 3-6% for two minutes at level ground pace. Then recover for two minutes by slow jogging and repeat the hill again. Recover for two minutes and repeat the hill again. Recover and run one minute on the hill and then repeat for one minute and finish out the workout with a cooldown of two miles easy. Remember the stretch after warmup and immediately after the end of the session.

Each week will require an increase of the hill angle and add thirty seconds to the uphill portions. So, by the eighth week of the Resistance Phase, the runner will have a typical workout consisting of two miles of warmup, then 8x4 minutes at an average of 5-6% with a one and one half minute recovery between each hill. Then, the runner will cool down with two miles of easy jogging. Additionally, the speed of the uphill portions will increase. If the athlete has started by running the uphill at 7:30 per mile pace on week one, the athlete should be able to comfortably run under 7:00 per mile uphill by week eight. Elite runners will run these repeats faster, of course. But, the runner should monitor the pace to make sure they do not become anaerobic during the uphill portion. However, the pace should be one that is fast enough to require strong, but controlled, effort. By week six, the last two repeats of the uphill should be very close to, but just under, anaerobic pace. This ensures the athlete has finished out the Phase at full effort. Below is an example of a typical Hobby runner Strength/Resistance week and the Elite runner week.

AVERAGE HOBBY STRENGTH SESSION WEEK

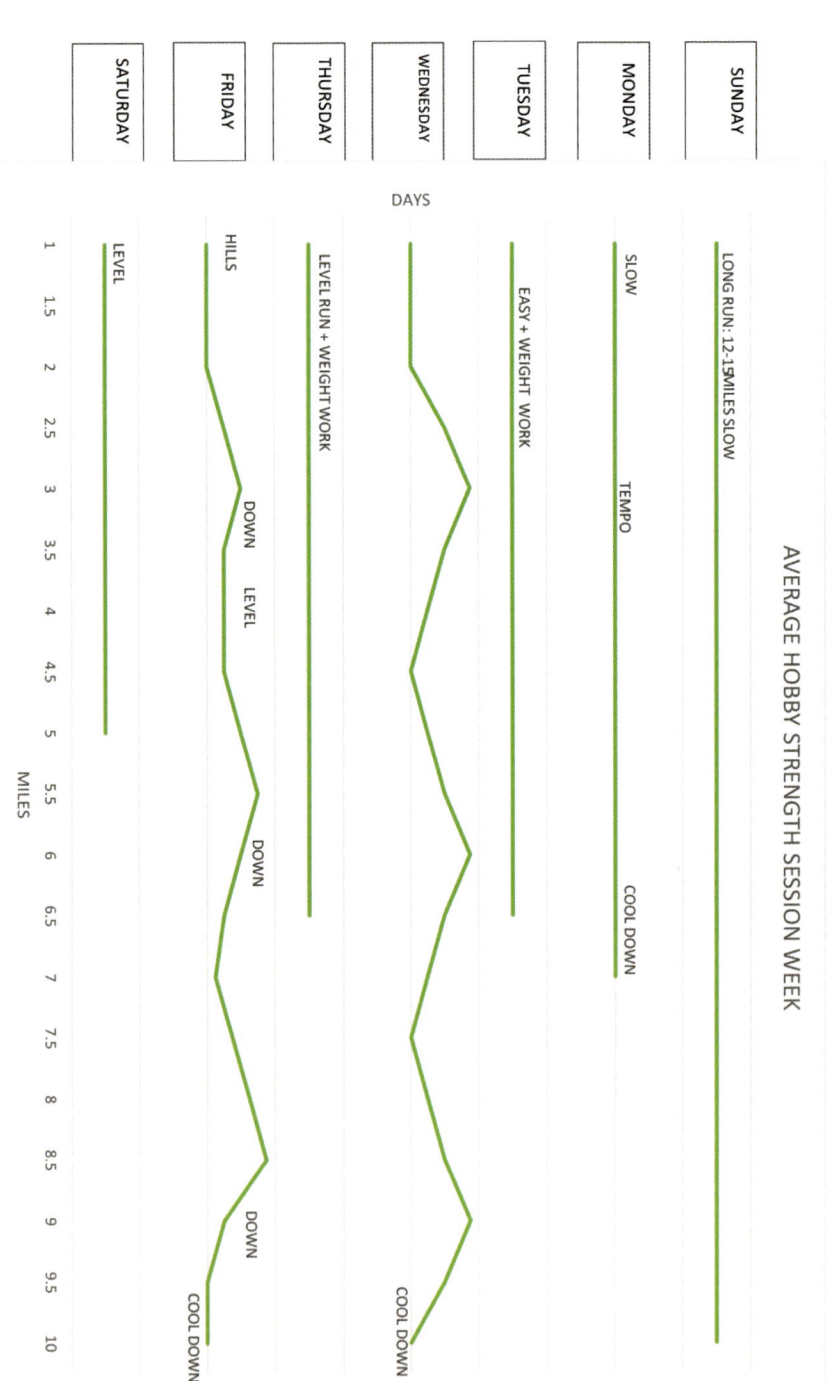

DAYS

SUNDAY	LONG RUN: 12-13 MILES SLOW
MONDAY	SLOW — TEMPO — COOL DOWN
TUESDAY	EASY + WEIGHT WORK — COOL DOWN
WEDNESDAY	COOL DOWN
THURSDAY	LEVEL RUN + WEIGHT WORK
FRIDAY	HILLS — DOWN — LEVEL — DOWN — DOWN — COOL DOWN
SATURDAY	LEVEL

MILES: 1 1.5 2 2.5 3 3.5 4 4.5 5 5.5 6 6.5 7 7.5 8 8.5 9 9.5 10

Notice Wednesday and Friday include 'hills' for resistance, noted by incline lines.
The Hobby runner will run their hills at 7:30 to 9:00 per mile on the Wednesday and Friday workouts and the inclines should average 5%.

94

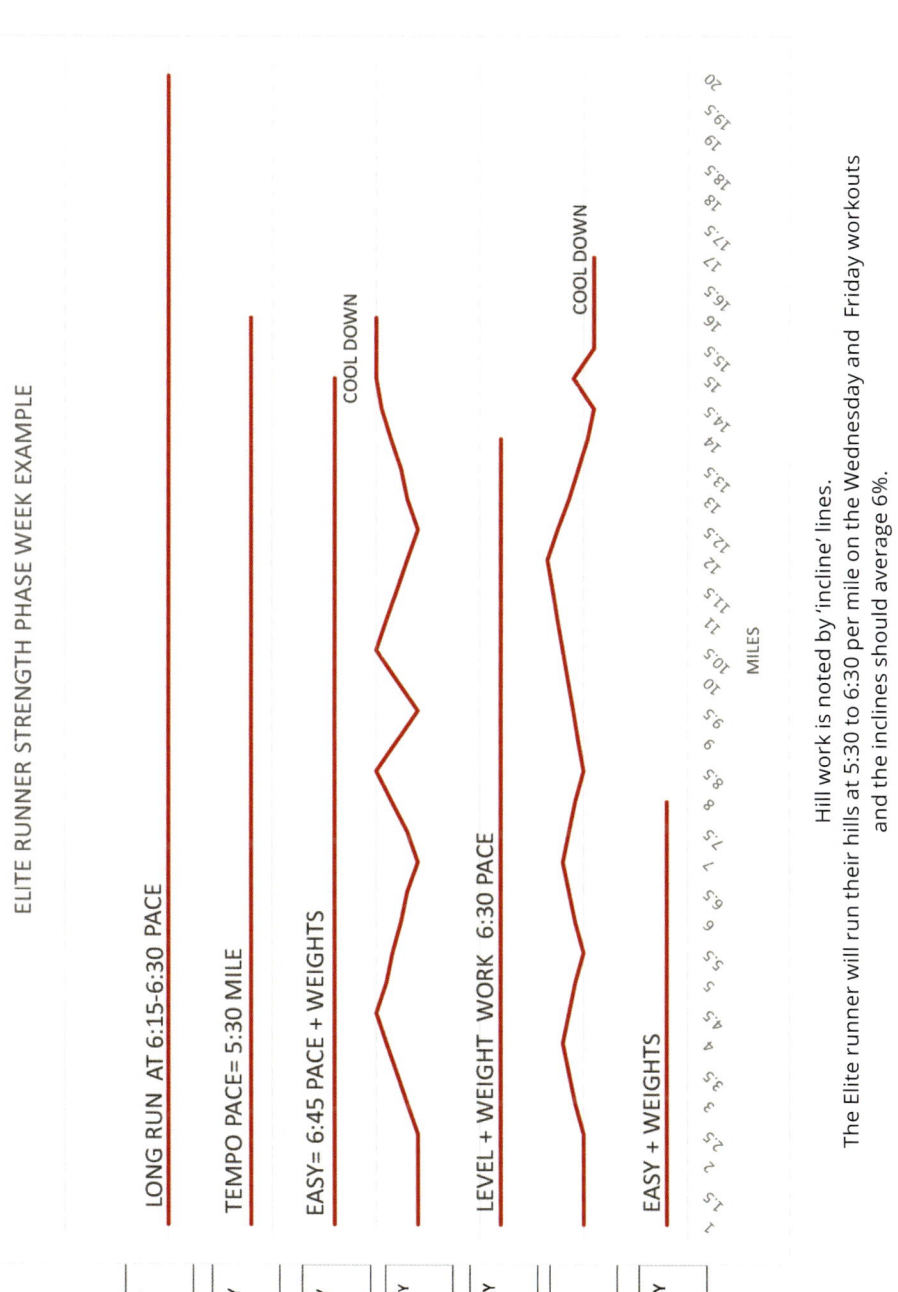

ELITE RUNNER STRENGTH PHASE WEEK EXAMPLE

SUNDAY — LONG RUN AT 6:15-6:30 PACE

MONDAY — TEMPO PACE= 5:30 MILE

TUESDAY — EASY= 6:45 PACE + WEIGHTS

WEDNESDAY — COOL DOWN

THURSDAY — LEVEL + WEIGHT WORK 6:30 PACE

FRIDAY — COOL DOWN

SATURDAY — EASY + WEIGHTS

MILES

1 1.5 2 2.5 3 3.5 4 4.5 5 5.5 6 6.5 7 7.5 8 8.5 9 9.5 10 10.5 11 11.5 12 12.5 13 13.5 14 14.5 15 15.5 16 16.5 17 17.5 18 18.5 19 19.5 20

Hill work is noted by 'incline' lines.
The Elite runner will run their hills at 5:30 to 6:30 per mile on the Wednesday and Friday workouts and the inclines should average 6%.

At the end of the Strength/Resistance phase, the runner will be equipped to shift gears again to the next and final preparation segment. Blood chemistry has changed, the lungs and heart are phenomenally stronger and the runner is ready. If the athlete has again been patient and diligent in the strength phase, it is time to roll into the section the runner yields for. Speed building.

REVIEW OF RESISTANCE PHASE:

The Strength/Resistance Phase is designed to begin the process of strengthening the quadriceps, waking up the fast twitch muscle cells and preparing the athlete for the latter stages of a race, where fatigue must be minimalized. The Distance Phase built the endurance for long runs. Adding in the strength this section provides, prepares the athlete to be not only highly endurance trained, but also ready to begin the approach to hyper fast running. Running hills, increasing weight work and speeding up the tempo pace has now added extra armament to a well-balanced muscle and mental system. We have now prepared ourselves for the fun. Fast running.

CHAPTER THREE

BUILDING SPEED

The next piece of the puzzle of the training season is the Speed Work Phase. Speed work refines the runner's ability to hold extreme anaerobic or high rate aerobic speed, with or without the ability of the lungs to supply oxygen at a rate to prevent the rapid buildup of lactic acid. It would seem this training section would be rather futile, as many marathon focused runners feel "I am not a good sprinter". This may be true to a certain extent, but leg strength and turnover can be improved in a surprisingly shorter number of weeks than the distance and strength phases. And speed is actually defined by the ability to increase leg turnover rate, increased efficient stride length and more powerful push off each foot plant. These can be improved in every runner. Using speed work as part of the overall training system of a higher caliber runner also increases the speed one can hold more comfortably, during any race from 800 meters to the marathon. That is the good news. The bad news is that two to three interval or fast tempo workouts per week, while maintaining high mileage can be a recipe for injury, if the athlete has not properly trained through the first two sections and rested enough, maintained flexibility, proper nutrition and hydration and all the other previous recommendations. But, this section is absolutely the one that will separate the good from the great. It will, at times, seem brutal, particularly during the first three weeks. Do not despair. If you finish this section, you will become comfortable with speed work and want more, not less. But, use speed work in a very structured manner. A poorly planned approach to this regimen has the ability to wreck a great deal of preparation.

During this final building phase for the long distance runner, the fast workouts will start out with long repetitions and gradually decrease in distance, as the runner 'tunes' their speed. They are better equipped for this after months of distance training, where the runner ran from 80-90% of their mileage in their comfort zone. Their strength has been increased now, as well. The distance of the fast sessions will start with speed/endurance repeats of up to four to five one mile repeats at 85-90% of full mile speed and work down to repeat two hundred meter sprints through the course of six to eight weeks. Additionally, there will be faster tempo runs of three to seven miles included in the speed work training. The tempo runs included in the early phases were to train the body to shift gears from comfortable to mildly uncomfortable pace, without distress. We now will zero in on the fast twitch fiber, in order to make a complete distance racer. This is all about coordinating the speed, endurance, handling of lactic acid, stride length and control of form into an efficient racer's body, without injuring the muscle and ligament/tendon groups. As the runner im-proves during this segment, two possible things can happen, though. First, the runner will become faster or second, the runner will become injured. Additionally, the form of the fast runner must become efficient enough to overcome lateral forces and provide the most kinetic force possible with the least wasted lateral movement. As the distance of the speed section shortens, the foot plant moves more force to the front of the foot. This will become easier to get used to as the run-ner becomes more experienced. A key benefit provided by the structured fast repetitions, is learning of how to instinctively know your pace at any point in a race or in training, for that matter. Any runner, who does not know the pace he or she is running, will experience less success. One must learn where the fine point of maximum aerobic pace transitions into the anaerobic realm. If this section is done properly, one will un-derstand how to use strategy in racing, to maximum advan-tage. If at the beginning of this phase, the runner can only run at 95% maximum speed for 200 meters and at the end of the phase, can hold that pace for 600 to 1,000 meters, think of the advantage gained for racing. Great milers to marathoners have this tool in their belt. It can make the difference between running down a competitor, or in holding the lead to the tape. Another benefit the runner will gain is the knowledge and abil-ity to use "negative splits" to their advantage. Every record set in distances from 200 meters to the marathon that I know of, has been set with negative splits involved. This is defined as running the second half of the race even faster than the first half. In fact, if one expects to become a high level marathoner, they better learn this concept and train for it.

The hardest issue to address and control in coaching long distance athletes during this phase, is holding them back and teaching them control. It is fun to run fast and after months of slower long runs, it is a welcomed change. However, the building of speed keeps the body on the edge and going too fast too soon, may result in long term traumatic muscle and tendon injury. Speed is built through the combination the several systems and kinetic movement addressed, working together at a high rate. If the previous sections have been ignored or a shortcut has been taken, the athlete is set up for potential disaster. This may sound a bit scary, but a severely torn hamstring or over stretched tendon can take the athlete away from the game for months. The vast majority of overuse injuries are repairable, but they may involve physical rehabilitation and in the worst case scenario, surgery may be required.

The reason to adamantly address the precise nature of learning to run fast without injury is to convince the athlete to respect the Speed Phase and the very fast intervals one will be doing in the final weeks of preparation to finely tune the training to the Peak Phase.

Intervals/Versus Steady Rate Speed

What type of speed is most efficient for the runner set on becoming a high caliber five thousand meter to the marathon, athlete? Both steady state speed (fast tempo) and intervals (shorter, repetitive fast sections with structured recovery between each) are very effective, but have some differences in what they are designed to achieve. We have already begun to gently wake up the fast twitch fiber with the tempo and hill runs included in the Distance and Strength Phases. The issue to address now is the race distance the runner will focus upon. The distance, speed and number of repetitions will be addressed specifically, in the sections on the Miler, the 5,000 Meter Runner, the 10,000 Meter Runner and the Marathon, for they all vary slightly according to the race distance of focus. Up to now, much of the training has been the same for the 1,500 or mile, 5k, 10k and the marathon. Now, the different races will separate in the type of training required in the speed sessions.

First, we will design the general training segments and focus for the hobby runner, moving to the elite runner or the serious runner who is working to get to the top in the five thousand meter to marathon distances. A guide for the first week and moving to the final week will be provided here. The key word here is "guide". Remember, George Sheehan said we are all an experiment of one. But, this is a guide to eliminate the day to day clutter of the 'workout of the week' mentality. We are concerned with the science of the sections and why each section is done in its particular order.

As the athlete begins to use high speed repetitions, the upper body work we have done will prove to be of great assistance in acceleration and maintaining higher speeds for longer distances. The arms and shoulders are critical to efficient cadence and the legs will want to move in unison with the arms. See the section on using free weights and stationary resistance machine strength improvement to understand specific work for runner efficiency.

To give one an example of how the distance runner's body is different even after weight work and speed work, from a high caliber sprinter, take a look at the best of the elite 100 meter sprinters. They have incredible quadriceps size and strength and high definition upper body strength. This is not for show. These athletes will be calling on all fast-twitch fiber and the ability to perform incredible leg turnover rate. The type of training a sprinter does will create more muscle hypertrophy, as opposed to speed work for distance athletes.

In a high caliber one hundred meter race, explosive speed is activated to get to maximum speed (over 27 miles per hour or better!) in less than 12 steps. This means the arms, shoulders and legs will all go to work at 100% potential at once. The system sprinters are using is the lactic acid system. High oxygen consumption is not the goal here. They are going totally anaerobic from start to finish. You will notice even the elite sprinter will be in total oxygen deficit at the finish line. An inexperienced observer might ask why the athlete is breathing so hard after only 100 or 200 meters of racing. Well, the athlete is essentially being suffocated in the cells during this race. So, recovery takes a little while. The body is working hard to oxygenate the cells, eliminate CO_2 and reduce the high buildup of lactic acid after such an effort, hence the heavy breathing for several minutes after the race.

The distance runner's speed work is very different from the sprinter. The distance runner will use speed, but not only does the typical high caliber marathoner not possess the speed of the sprinter, but is looking for a different balance of using oxygen as fuel and anaerobic speed, using the lactic acid system to supplement the endurance increased during the previous segments. The distance athlete seeks to train the body to call on different systems at different phases of the race.

Distance Runner Speed and Its Cellular Complexity

The weekly set of workouts will absolutely change from the Strength/Resistance Phase to the six to eight weeks of Speed workouts to develop the maximum speed a runner is capable to hold. We have learned, as early as the Distance Phase that some athletes will possess higher levels of fast twitch fiber than others and some will have a higher ratio of slow twitch fiber. Here again, we see a form of natural selection coming into play for the best distance suited for the athlete to race. A sprinter is a sprinter and a distance runner is a distance runner and never the twain shall meet, (except nearing a finish line). An exception to this rule is the fact that many milers move up to the longer races as they age, due to the fact that they no longer have quite the spark to run a 3:45 to 3:50 mile, but they still have much more raw speed than their fellow competitors when they move to a 5k, 10k or marathon. Their stride length is longer and their turnover rate in their legs is faster than the long distance guys and girls, so they run faster more comfortably and frequently have great success. I think of the great New Zealand miler, Rod Dixon, who decided to move up to the marathon for a change and ran a new world record at the time of a little over 2:08 and won the New York City Marathon.

Looking at what we have learned so far, it would seem at times, that working to increase speed is fruitless if one is a distance runner and equally fruitless to work to maximize endurance in a sprinter. However, we have learned also, that the systems can be improved in each athlete, due to the adaptability of the human skeletal muscle cells.The fact that we seek to increase speed during this phase, factors like leg turnover and stride length begin to become more important. This is precisely why we have taken the athlete through these sections in a structured schedule. Speed is simply increasing leg turnover rate and stride length at the same time. Leg turnover and increased stride length means flexibility becomes even more important and different types of energy systems will be called upon. As a runner begins to accelerate, the quadriceps are used to extend the leg and push the body and the hamstrings are used to flex the leg on each stride and increase turnover in preparation for the next foot strike. If this sounds complex, it is. But, the issue the runner needs to be concerned with is muscle strength, muscle balance and endurance. We have already worked through the Distance Phase and the

Strength Phase. Now we want to fine tune this machine to hold high speeds for long distances.

Let's take a look at the additional sessions the highly trained runner will use in this final segment of the training process. This training system will have some workouts that never change (except after a major race), during the entire year. The long run will always be a staple of the system. In addition, the moderately long, brisk run will always remain. So, what changes and when?

After the buildup of distance, general training pace will increase, due to increased ability to oxygenate the muscles, as a result of the adaptations mentioned earlier. Athletes become more comfortable at a higher training pace after four or more months of endurance buildup. The second phase, focusing on endurance and strength together, toughens the runner for different terrains and also seeks to produce better anterior and posterior muscle balance. Secondarily, the upper body is given more attention in that section, in order to help maintain form, keep arm cadence consistent and increase the ability of the abdominals and intercostal muscles to help 'pull' the diaphragm down with each breath, thus filling the lungs with more air.

The speed building section does this, as well as helping to provide a greater array of muscles available for speed in the 1,500 meters to the 5,000 meters and supplementing both speed and strength in the latter stages of distances up to the marathon.

This is yet another facet to consider. The key to all of this is performing the correct workouts during the right phase, resting and stretching properly and receiving proper nutrition and fluids during all of the above. But, if one wants to make sure all of this is maximized, accountability in the form of a training partner or coach is extremely helpful. It is very easy to talk oneself out of a tough workout. But, it is much tougher to look your training partner or coach in the eye and say, "I don't feel like it today". If you can, try to have a running partner of equal or slightly higher ability, to maintain motivation and accountability.

Week One of Speed-Work Phase for the Hobby Distance Runner Racing 5 and 10k:

Day One:
Run 12-14 miles at an easy pace. Stretch lightly at two miles and immediately upon completion of the workout.

Day Two:
Warmup with 2 miles very easy, then run a normal, comfortable pace for 5 miles. Do a set of curls, presses, crunches and 'flys'. Stretch, as described above. This is a recovery day.

Day Three:
This is a track day. Warmup for 2 miles, lightly stretch and then begin 3x1 mile at 80% of your top mile ability. By the sixth

week, these repetitions will all increase. You will, according to the preferred distance you have chosen, go up to 4 or 5x one mile for this particular set. And they all will be faster, with less recovery. You can find out pretty quickly what your top mile speed is, by warming up on the first day of speed work and running a mile as fast as you can. If your fastest mile is 6:00, then 80% of that figure can be calculated, as 360 seconds plus 72 seconds (or 20% added to your 6:00 time). So, in this scenario, one would run repeat miles in about 7:12 each. Recover 800 meters in between each fast mile, by very slow jogging (10 minute miles). Cool down with 2 miles at an easy pace similar to the normal warmup pace. Please note that many times, the recovery will mean the athlete is starting the next fast section at a point other than the start/finish line. Learn the track's markers and you will become more comfortable with this as you gain experience. Watching and noting the meter lines on a track as you run your repeats, will help you to make each fast section consistent and will have the added effect of aiding the athlete in instinctively knowing his or her pace in a race. Knowing precise pace is critical to effective and successful racing. And notice that I have not recommended or suggested the 400 meter track in the previous two sections. The reason for this is simple. The track teaches the athlete how to run precise pace and increase that pace over time, by knowing what each pace feels like. The stride length is lengthened and the arm swing must be increased to stay in cadence with pace. Arm swing and leg turnover are directly correlated, particularly when running fast.

Day Four:

This is a rest day, consisting of 6 miles easy, a long stretching session and yoga or other meditative/relaxation techniques. Do some easy weights and core strengthening, using crunches, as in the Tuesday workout. Stretching after weight work is also important. So, though I do not mean to harp on it, do it.

Day Five:

Warmup with 2 miles easy and then move into a fartlek session of approximately three minutes at 5k race pace then slow to normal pace for two minutes. Repeat. Then, move into two minutes at slightly faster than 5k race pace (10 seconds per mile faster). Repeat. Then, cool down with enough easy running to accrue 12 total miles. This day is done on the roads, not the track.

Day Six:

Warmup for 2 miles, then stretch lightly. Do 6-8 'striders' of 100 meters each. This is a light sprint designed to wake up the fast twitch fiber and literally stride lengthen the athlete. When one does striders, the athlete should practice lengthening stride and preparing the leg muscles for longer strides and higher leg turnover. At the completion of this, run 6x800 meters at ten seconds per mile faster than 5k race pace. By week six, you will be going up to 30 seconds per mile better than your 5k pace. Recover between each 800 with three minutes of very slow jogging. Then, proceed to cool down with 3 miles of easy running. This session should produce about 10 miles for the day. This is a track workout, as far as the repeats are concerned. The warmup and cooldown can move to the roads.

Day Seven:
This is another recovery day. Run 8 to 10 miles easy. Stretch and relax with yoga or meditation. No weight work is absolutely necessary, but as your fitness increases, you may want to put in a light weight session on this day.

This example schedule has produced about 70 miles for the week. The well trained and higher level marathoner will want to supplement this mileage with doing an additional set of easy miles in the morning if the runner does the main workout in the evening, or in the evening if the athlete's main workout is done in the morning, and the sets will be faster, of course. We briefly discussed this in the high level distance phase. The well trained runner can handle double workouts three or four times a week and their fast repeats will be longer initially, and faster. This is the way to do 100+ mile weeks, even in the speed phase of training toward a peak. The eight or so, hours between workouts is enough time for the high caliber runner to recover and lactic acid levels to return to normal.

As with the strength phase, you see some light weight work is advisable to maintain core balance However, I do not recommend leg weights or leg machine work during the speed phase of a marathoner or a 10k specialist. There are two reasons behind this. First, there is the risk of muscle tears in the legs at this point in the schedule. Second, the speed itself is now activating the quadriceps and gastrocnemius groups, so leg weights are not needed during the buildup of speed for the distance runner. This will, however, be something the elite miler uses, as he or she has a different ratio of slow to fast twitch fiber and due less mileage accrual, overall. Anterior and posterior muscle balance is extremely important here and the upper body and core abdominal groups are much less likely to suffer injury, if the runner is smart about the 'high rep, low weight' philosophy.

Week 8 of Hobby Runner Speedwork

At week eight in the Hobby runner Speed Phase, the fast sections you will notice, work down to 400 meter repeats and 200 meter repeats, just as they would in an elite athlete. Here is a typical week eight schedule for this level runner:

Day One:
Run 18 miles at a pace that is now noticeably faster than when you started this phase. For instance, due to the fact you have taught the body's muscle memory to respond more quickly and hold higher pace longer, all other workouts will now be easier and faster. The long 18 mile day may now average 15-20 seconds per mile faster than when you entered the phase. In fact, it will be faster after phase two and faster yet, after phase three. This is expected, but just a word of caution here: There

is a saying, "Don't leave your race on the training road". That is, remember exactly what each workout's desired effect is to be and do not turn training into races, especially when training with a partner or group. This remarkably easy to do, as we are racers and a challenge, either intentional or just because someone feels particularly good that day, is hard to back away from. There is no reason to risk six months to a year of training just because you know you can normally outrun someone in a race.

Day Two:
Warm up for 2 miles then stretch and run 4 more miles at a comfortably easy pace. But, this is a light day, so treat it that way. Do another round of stretching immediately after the run. Try to start adding meditative disciplines after each workout if you have not already, but especially after the main hard or long workouts. To train the mind to relax as a matter of daily life, will be of great assistance in tamping down the pre-race jitters that waste energy and tighten already somewhat tight muscles. The athlete who can turn off the jitters, somewhat, will learn to remain patient in races and more ready to strike when the time is right. Weights and core exercises should be used on this day, also.

Day Three:
Warm up two miles and then stretch. Run 8x400 meters at thirty seconds per mile faster than 5k race pace. Now note, that the athlete's 5k race pace is faster than it was several

months ago, so if one has difficulty figuring what pace these should be, use heartrate. If your maximum heartrate is 195 for a 25 year old, then 175 beats per minute will give the athlete 90% of max. After an athlete has spent years in the sport, the maximum heartrate will most likely be higher, as described in the 'Alarmed Researcher Story'. This is a good place to start, however. If it takes more than 90-100 seconds to recover to 100 to 110 beats per minute, the runner is going too fast. This correlation works well, but read your body. As you get more miles under your belt, you will understand what your pace should be. After three or four weeks of doing 400 meter intervals, it will become instinctive. This accomplishes more than just teaching the body to run faster with less stress. It teaches pace, period. If the athlete cannot run 8-10 repetitions by week eight of the speed phase, extend the phase by two weeks and slow by three to five seconds per repetition. Most likely, this will not be the case. If all other phases have been followed properly, there is no reason one should not be able to complete this and all the other weeks of speed sessions. You may have noticed, that at week one of the speed section, you were doing not just longer repetition distances, but you were running at closer to 80-85% of your VO2 max for them. You will now be doing repetitions at 5-10% higher VO2 max. As the athlete has moved through this entire training system, the ability of the lungs to absorb oxygen has increased, the use of this oxygen has become more efficient and the supplementary systems used in anaerobic running have improved. We have worked to train the whole body and all of its muscle systems.

The reasoning behind this 'periodization' training, as Arthur Lydiard called it, plus the additional information available to enhance training that we now have, makes training more efficient, definitive and lessens the chance of injury. After the 8-10 fast 400 meter sections have been completed, cool down with two miles easy and stretch.

Day Four:
This is another recovery day. We are focusing on quality work on the hard days and recovery on the alternate days. We are actually doing this all through the system, but it is especially important when high speed running comes into play. So, warmup with very easy running for 2 miles, then gently finish with 5-6 miles of comfortable running. Stretch and meditate. Do the core and weight exercises on this day, as well.

Day Five:
Warm up for 2 miles and then stretch. Then, ease into a light fartlek session of two minutes at 80% and slow down to a comfortable pace. Go up to 85% for three minutes and down again for three minutes. Go up to five minutes at 80% and then down again. Repeat this for a second round and then finish off for a total of 12 miles. If the runner wants to substitute tempo for the fartlek, it is acceptable, but may bring on some staleness, so use caution if this alternative is chosen. Stretch and meditate.

Day Six:

Warm up for two miles and then stretch. Go into your 'striders', with at least six to ten of them. Now, you will do 8x200 meters, with one minute between each, ideally. If you require a few more seconds for recovery, so be it. The 200 meter sections are now at 90% max. If you have an accurately measured straight 200 meter distance, this is great. Running track curves without a significant level of experience can open one up to accidental injury. So, use care and hold form through the fast sections. If no one at the track objects, I recommend you do 4 in the traditional counterclockwise direction and 4 clockwise. If you stay to the outside of the track, the curve is more gently turned, so this tip may help avoid injury, as well. Track etiquette is to be practiced at all times. Never get in the way of a faster runner or barge in to a team working out. You may get permanently banned from using a track if this happens enough and once can be enough. Cool down with 3-5 miles easy. Stretch and meditate.

Day Seven:

This will be a recovery day. Get in an easy 3 in the morning and 5-7 in the evening and practice your disciplines discussed above. This 'two-a- day' workout technique can even be used on 'easy' days to get the miles in. The elite runner will begin week one with repeat miles on one speed day and repeat 800's on the other speed day. By week eight, the elite runner will do repeat 400's on one speed day and repeat 200's on the other. The repeat miles in week one will be 5x1 mile at 4:50 to

5:00 pace and the 800's will be at 8x800 at 4:45 per mile pace. At week eight, the pace will still be 4:40 per mile for the 400's, but the 200's will be at 30 seconds each, or 4:00 mile pace. The elite runner is usually able to handle a tempo day in addition to the track days. An elite runner may run 8-10 miles at a 5:30 pace tempo and still not become stale. By the time a runner has attained the ability to handle 100+ mile weeks, they have this type of strength. The Hobby Runner's workouts are perhaps a bit slower, but one day they may well have that 'elite runner' tag, so though I talk about the elite runner's workouts through much of this, think of it as your goal, if you are not there yet.

The chart on the following page is an example of a typical week for both the Elite and the Hobby runner during the Speed Phase, but it will not match the above written schedules exactly. This is because it will change during the six to eight weeks you are in it and the fartlek day will go away near the end of the section, to be replaced by shorter, faster structured interval repeats.

ELITE RUNNER

SUNDAY	MONDAY	TUESDAY	WEDNESDAY	THURSDAY	FRIDAY	SATURDAY
LONG RUN 20-22 MILES AT 6:00-6:15 PACE	EASY DAY AT 7:00 PACE	WARMUP 2 MILES THEN 5x 1 MILE AT 5:00 TO 4:50 PACE	EASY RUN OF 15 MILES AT 6:30 TO 7:00 PACE	WARMUP 2 MILES THEN 16x 400m AT 4:40 PACE THEN COOL DOWN 2 MILES	EASY RUN AT 7:00 PACE	WARMUP 2 MILES THEN TEMPO PACE FOR 8 MILES, TEN COOL DOWN 2 MILES
22	8	12 - 14	15 - 17	10 - 12	15	12

94 TO 100 MILES

HOBBY RUNNER

SUNDAY	MONDAY	TUESDAY	WEDNESDAY	THURSDAY	FRIDAY	SATURDAY
LONG RUN 18 MILES AT 8:00 PACE	EASY RUN 6 MILES AT 8:00 PACE	WARMUP 2 MILES SLOW THEN 3x 800m AT 6:00 MILES THEN COOL DOWN	WARMUP 2 MILES SLOW THEN NORMAL 8:00 PACE FOR 6 MORE MILES	WARMUP 2 MILES SLOW THEN 6x 400m AT 5:50 TO 6:00 PACE	EASY RUN AT 8:00 PACE	STEADY STATE WITH TEMPO MIDDLE 3 MILES AT 6:30 PACE
18 - 20	6 OR 7	6	8 OR 10	6 OR 7	8 OR 10	10

62 TO 70 MILES

THE ALTHETE SHOULD STRETCH PROPERLY AFTER EACH WORKOUT BEFORE MUSCLES COOL DOWN TO NORMAL.

Using Meditation Techniques:
During these speed section weeks, resting mind and body becomes not only as necessary as in the othe Phases, but is absolutely critical in order to relax the muscle systems and mind to the point that the runner has done all they can to stay not only maximally fit, but highly relaxed and loose.This discipline does not have to be done at any particular time of the day or evening, but it should be a daily part of your training. We now know enough about meditation and yoga and other flexibility/relaxation techniques, to understand they have a tremendously positive effect on the health and performance of athletes and anyone, for that matter. I have mentioned it several times in this book for a reason. Athletes tend to focus on the workout and forget the not so little things that can give them an edge. Meditation doesn't take a track, a road or even shoes to be practiced. If you haven't a person to teach you this important discipline, buy a book on it or ask a friend who practices it, to help you.

We will now address specifics. I am many times asked what correct form means. Form changes as speed changes, but there is the ideal form and then there is the reality of individual forms.

Tapering for Racing

The Taper Phase is different for all race distances. It is essentially the last Phase of training to race. The knowledge of how to taper correctly is key, to being completely ready for a race. To use the marathon as the standard for an example of tapering, a reduction in both mileage and effort should begin ten days out from the race. The runner will back up the dates from the race day and begin to ease off the pedal, so to speak, in order to achieve two things.

First, the reduction in mileage, assuming nutrient quality and density has been maintained, will start amassing the maximum amount of glycogen in the cells. In the past, it was thought prudent to "carbohydrate load". This is not necessary, however, if the athlete is using less glycogen on a daily basis during the taper and merely maintaining the amount of daily glycogen intake necessary to handle 80-100 miles per week during training and do normal work. Most high endurance athletes will take in from 3,500 to up to 5,000 calories per day, during high mileage weeks and will still maintain ideal body weight. Elite marathoners, as was stated earlier in this book, will typically be of very low body fat, proportionally for sex, than the sedentary or even middle distance runner. However, they are still required to consume more calories than a normal human, just to maintain. For example, I had a body fat measurement of 1.5% when I was running up to 100 miles per week. My weight was approximately 132 pounds and my height is 5'10'. I was very strong for that weight, as my muscle mass was high and body fat low.

The marathoner will still do many of the same workouts they were doing during the speed work phase, while reducing the distances and speed, during this taper. The long run will come down to 15-17 miles at day T (-10). Day nine will be the usual recovery day of 6-8 miles. T (-8) will be 8 x 400 meters along with the warmup and cooldown. Notice the reduction in the number of repeats here. Additionally, instead of running them at say, 72 seconds each, they will be run at 76-78 seconds each. So, the effort has been reduced. Day T (-7) will be a steady state effort of 65-70% VO2 max for 10-12 miles. Day T (-6) will be 8 miles easy. Day T (-5) will see a warmup of 1.5 miles, the 6 x 200 at 80% usual 200 meter effort. This helps to keep the legs fresh and yet lets the fast twitch muscle memory continue to activate later on. Day T (-4) will be 5 miles easy. Day T (-3) will be 3-4 miles easy. Day T (-2) will be 2-3 easy and slow, with stretching emphasis and higher fluid intake. It takes 48 hours, depending on the starting level of hydration, to reach maximal hydration, especially for runners training in hot climates. Additionally, it should be noted that while the runner is not 'carbo loading' during this time, four grams of water are necessary to store one gram of glycogen and up to nine grams of water are needed to store and activate fat into ATP for potential energy sources. Electrolyte balance should be accentuated during all training, but should be complete before toeing the starting line. Day T (-1) should be taken off, or just a mile or so run easy, with mild stretching, just to keep loose.

Tapering for the shorter races is important, but not as complex. Just easing up on the overall mileage from four to five days out and eliminating the normal last speed session for the week of the race is usually enough to rest the legs and remain properly hydrated.

The athlete may feel a bit 'full' during this taper and may even gain a pound or two, of weight. But, this will be most likely due to water and nutrient intake pre-race. This is a delicate subject, but we should also address race day preparation. First, hopefully the runner will eliminate waste properly all the time, but this is especially important early on race day. No one wants to have to make a 'pit stop' during the race or have an accident. However, make sure water and electrolyte intake is maintained before the race. Having a meal before the race is not necessary, as it will take six hours to assimilate solid nutrients and eliminate waste products. Besides, the athlete should have their nutrient intake completed by race day, anyway. Some athletes will want to have a small snack or energy bar before a race, but this will only temporarily raise blood glucose. Still, if this is a normal training pattern, it shouldn't hurt and at least may help psychologically, for pre-race routine. Just make sure fluid intake is kept up. Having to urinate just before a race is a good sign.

During distances of 10k to the marathon, runners may want to take in water during the race for two reasons. First, cool water helps to keep core temperature down. Second, water that is approximately 45 degrees Fahrenheit will be absorbed fairly quickly and slow the inevitable dehydration from running 26+

miles hard. One will never keep up with the loss of fluid during the race, but slowing this process can be very helpful, especially near the end of the race. Runners can lose up to six to seven pounds of water (nearly a gallon) during a marathon. To run a good marathon, the athlete doesn't have the time or ability to replace this amount during of fluid. It is a good idea to practice fluid intake during training runs, so the athlete will be used to taking water in, on the run. Bill Rodgers routinely came to a complete stop to drink water in marathons, as he was not comfortable drinking while running. The good effects of taking in the fluid certainly outweighed the time lost for the water stop. It didn't hurt him, apparently, as he ran many of the best races in America using his method.

But, in order to prepare to run the best times possible, practice running and scooping up a cup of water or your pre mixed bottle of electrolyte replacement drink and sipping it as you go. Trying to throw it all down your throat at one time will most likely result in choking on the fluid and losing time trying to regain composure.

Peaking properly and for the longest time possible requires a change in behavior. Resting the night after a race, replacing carbohydrates within four to six hours and straddling a fine line between resting too much and training too hard during the race period is a difficult lesson to learn. Even when peaking for races, there will be some fast training and some long runs in between races, in order to maintain the maximum oxygen uptake and fast runs to keep the fast twitch fiber 'awake'.

Form at Different Speeds

I have seen some really ugly form in distance runners. And yet ironically, some of these athletes were very successful. However, efficient form helps the runner use less energy and a straight line usually gets one to the end faster. The arms should be carried with the elbow bent at a 90 degree angle and should not cross the center line of the body. The shoulders should remain relaxed, though they are in use. The term relaxed in this context, means keeping the trapezoid groups as loose as possible, while performing arm swing. Form is something the athlete can actively work to improve, just like any of the other training and racing sections. Distance runners need to be able to carry the upper body for up to three hours or more, while maintaining good kinetic form. During the long runs, form will reveal itself. The balanced musculature of a well-trained runner will enhance the ability to 'shift gears' and remain relaxed. The quadriceps will extend the legs to an imaginary line, straight through the shoulders, knees and down to the rear to mid-foot strike.

As the runner begins to use very high speeds, during track work, intervals or the final sprint to the finish line, knee lift will increase, as well as stride length. Since leg turnover will also increase, the runner may well find foot strike moving to the forefoot. This part of the kinesiology of proper fast pace form will need to definitely be practiced. Distance runners spend most of their time in anything but a sprint. Observe the incredible straight line movement in a sprinter. Every move, knee lift, arm swing and push off is designed to accomplish one thing. That thing is getting from point A to point B, with as little wasted lateral movement as possible. The distance runner should take note of the sprinter's straight line movement, but the longer distances will require less knee lift and there will be more upper body relaxation during the runs. The distance runner will also foot strike, most of the time, at the outside rear of the heel or a bit further up toward the mid-foot when speeding up. The sprinter also will have a slight forward lean, almost like they are falling forward. And actually, all running is the act of falling forward, with a push from front to rear and stabilization by the act of the forward foot hitting the ground under the shoulder. Please do not be discouraged if your form is not terrific. Some top runners had small idiosyncrasies in form, yet became fabulous performers despite the imperfect arm carry, outside leg swing and other types of odd styles, while blowing down the competition anyway. Practice good form, but don't force good form. Forcing a kinetic style change, may lead to injury.

Specific Distance Differences in Training
THE MILER

We have focused primarily on the athlete who seeks to become a great 5k, 10k or marathoner, so far. Well, what if a runner wants to focus on the mile and what factors determine if the athlete has elite mile potential? We will start with the miler, as the young runner usually has that distance available in middle and high school. The greatest milers are unique animals, who show signs of their ability at a fairly early age. That is why we do not lump the miler into the other distance regimens. Milers have a great deal of ability born into them. It just needs to be trained gently as a youngster then sharpened into a hard edge as an adult.

The miler has several differences, physically, from a marathoner and one difference is in their muscle cells themselves. He or she will have a ratio of 40% to nearly 50% fast twitch fiber, where the marathoner, as we discussed, will be closer to 20% fast twitch fiber. The mile, though seemingly short for a longer competitor, is an incredibly tough race. The factors that determine success in this race are intense focus and the ability to be a smart tactician, in addition to their speed. There is no time in the mile to lose focus. It is a race that uses both the lactic acid system and the oxygen system at the same time. The good miler has a tendency, therefore, to emerge and expose their talent at a pretty young age. Elite milers have the ability to run at 95% of their aerobic capacity for ¾ of a mile and then sprint at world class 200 meter speed for the last 200-400 yards. The mile is unlike any other race. The other most brutal race is the 800. If an athlete is very good at the 800, they have a good chance at moving to the mile later on.

A disclaimer here is required ethically I believe, to caution the parent who wants the athlete to be a good athlete in running or any other sport, for that matter. Runners tend to fall in love with the sport, rather than becoming part of a forced marriage, so to speak. The parent's job is to encourage the best, support the endeavor and help when they see the young athlete struggling. Seek to offer direction, but not pressure. Forcing a youngster to head out for a five or ten mile run, even if they are capable of this, is a recipe for the child falling out of love with this and most sports. This is not to say structure is a bad thing. Children look to parents for stability and structure. It actually comforts a child to know they have a source for direction. If the child exhibits the 'play' in the sport, mentioned at the beginning of this book, they may well desire to become excellent. If the child or adult wants to be the best in this game, a part time coach is a good idea. If you are reading this book, you will know what to look for in the selection of a coach to encourage the correct workouts at the correct time. Additionally, very young runners are still developing the long bones of the legs. Damage to growth plates may occur, if a child or adolescent is running too many miles. If you are concerned with this, consult a good sports physician. Children up to the age of about twelve should hold their mileage to about twenty to twenty five miles a week or less. Twenty-five is usually tolerated fairly well, as active children are running about that distance in play, anyway.

Now, if say a fourteen year old male or female wants to be a good miler, they will need base conditioning discussed in sections one and two, but on a reduced mileage schedule. Thirty miles a week is a lot for a person of this age. If the young person has a gotten to this stage, they are ready for a test. I cannot stress enough, that the sections of this program should be adhered to in order, before rushing into a test of fitness for a particular distance. Now, when I take on an adult runner, I use an initial mile time trial to determine how I will set up the program or change their current one, in order to build or re-build a runner for high level competition. I recommend using an 800 meter time trial to test the type of distance a young athlete may pick for focus. If the runner is a male and can cover this in less than three minutes after a good base has been established, they may have good mile potential. If the runner is female, three minutes to three minutes and twenty seconds may indicate a strong female miler is there to be developed. Never discourage the runner if they do not fall exactly in these time schedules, however. Everyone has a bad day and that may be theirs. If a young person has been identified with the potential for the mile, the training and base work discussed in the earlier specific sections, will be similar. However, we will see focus shifted from high mileage, to moderate mileage and strength and speed work will have a much higher ratio in the miler, as opposed to the marathoner.

The miler must stay conditioned with a good aerobic and strength base all year. The difference in the miler's training lies in the amount of speed work and weight training they must do to keep their high fast twitch ratio conditioned, while maintaining a good base. The miler will have typically, a longer stride length and a more 'muscled' look, due to the strength work they must do. Milers won't take on the look of the sprinter, however and the physical look of milers can vary within its own specific distance. Some great East African milers have the look of a marathoner. However, when their stride length is examined, therein one sees a key to their speed. Many of my African and some Northern European miler friends are very lean. They have learned to develop that incredible stride length that separates them literally, from the field. The miler is not looking for muscle hypertrophy, but highly conditioned fast twitch fiber, coupled with a very high VO2 max.

As noted, the miler must be able to hold a fine line between aerobic and anaerobic speed, so their base load for the first two phases will seldom go over 70-80 miles per week, but they are usually equipped to cover even their 'easy long runs' at a speed faster than a marathoner. Their strength phase is similar to the other race distance training schedules. But, when the miler gets to the speed section, they separate from the long distance runner.

The Miler runs with a marathoner story-

In our area, we used to have an elite road mile, similar to the Fifth Avenue Mile in New York City. It was called The King Street Mile and it was very fast in the elite male and female divisions. The elite male competitors could all run under four minutes for the mile. The elite females could all run around 4:30 or faster. I worked with this race and hosted some of the runners at my home. The winning times were usually in the low to mid 3:50's. Not bad. The day after the race, several of us would go for a run together. I was shocked to see some of the elites complain about the distance and pace. A few of us typically ran our six to ten mile training runs at 5:30 to 6:00 minutes per mile. Several of the elites had difficulty holding this pace for ten miles. This wasn't because they lacked the talent, but because they were 'peaking' for the mile, therefore their fast twitch fiber was very conditioned and though their VO2 max was very high, it was not ready for long, fast running. See the section on peaking to understand this concept. They had an increased lung capacity, high alveoli concentration and a great level of mitochondria. But, they were trained and peaking for the mile, not the marathon. Thus, they had some difficulty at longer distances. This is an example, though it may be anecdotal, of how the type of training one does, affects performance at other distances.

Peak Weeks Example for Hobby or High School Miler:

Day One
This is a distance day to work on VO2 uptake maintenance. Run an easy 7-8 miles at (6:30) mile pace. Then, usually six to eight hours later, a light weight workout of: military curls-8-10 repetitions of 15-20 pounds per hand, with 30 to 60 seconds recovery between each. Next, perform the military standing press with 20-30 pounds. Do three sets with 30-60 recovery between each set. Third, do a three set bench press session with 30- 40 pounds and 8-10 repetitions. Note, females are not locked into this weight. They will do the same workout, but with slightly lighter weight for some. Try to use the same

recovery times for all weight sets. Next will be three sets of 25 crunches. Finish the workout with an easy stretching session, focusing on both upper and lower body areas. Yoga is a very good way to work on both flexibility and mind calming at the same time.

Day Two

This is a longer strength/speed day. Warm up for two miles at a very slow and deliberate pace. Then, do 4 x 1320 meters at (5:00) pace with two minutes recovery time between each fast section. The recovery should be at a very slow jog. If, after two minutes, the heartrate has not returned to approximately 100-110 beats per minute, continue to jog for another minute. It is important to get the heartrate down and oxygen saturation up before beginning another set. After the sets are completed, jog two miles for a cool down and stretch. If one desires a meditative session later that day, it is highly encouraged. What we now know about training is the relaxation of the mind not only speeds recovery, but also rests the body and increases focus for racing.

Day Three

This is a heavy strength day. Begin the first session of the day, with a 4-5 mile run at an easy pace. The afternoon session will be the weight workout to build and maintain speed and fast twitch fiber. Start the session with a short warm up of slow jogging for 1-2 miles, then stretch. Begin the weight session with three sets of military curls of 15-20 pounds and 8-10 repetitions, with 30-60 seconds between each set. Next, perform three sets of military presses with 20-25 pounds with the same recovery time and the same number of repetitions. Next will be three sets of leg extensions. These will only be 30 degrees of extension with 20 pounds and 8-10 repetitions. It is extremely important to limit leg extensions to 30 degrees and no further. Going further than this can severely injure the knees. I am wary of using leg extension machines for distance runners, as it is easy to use too much weight and even easier to go past the 30 degree bend. After the leg bends past 40 degrees, the ligaments are involved, not the muscles. The knee ligaments can become over stretched can become so damaged, that surgery is required. Additionally, there is no more strength gained from going past 30 degrees of flexion. Next, will be three sets of crunches for the abdominals. Use 25 repetitions and go up to 30 repetitions if the session is too easy. Crunches keep the abdominals and lower back muscles in balance and prevent improper form and the development of 'sway back' in runners. Close out this workout with a two mile easy jog to help 'flush' lactic acid out from the weight session. Stretch.

Day Four

This is another distance day, but with a tweak. Run 7-8 miles, starting out slowly, but increasing each mile by 10 seconds per mile. For instance, if the first mile is 7:00 pace, the last mile will be at 5:40 pace. This is a negative split aerobic day. Stretch.

Day Five

Warmup with two miles easy, then stretch and do ten easy striders of 100 meters each. Then, the 'meat' of the workout will be 6x400 at 70 seconds each and then 4x200 at 26 seconds each. Cool down with two miles easy and stretching.

Day Six

This is an easy day. Run 4 miles in the a.m. and 4 miles in the p.m. at a comfortable pace of about 7:00 pace. Stretch and meditation should follow.

Day Seven

Run 8 to 10 miles and then a light weight workout to follow in the p.m. Do the normal series of sets, but reduce the weight by 5% on each set. Stretch and meditate.

During this phase, the runner should be starting to become comfortable with using negative splits, both in the distance days and on the track, as well. The good miler will need to be an athlete who can increase the pace throughout the entire race, until the 200-300 meter sprint to the finish.

Typical High Level Miler Schedule in the Peak Speed Phase:

-Base running for the week: 50-55 miles maximum at approximately 5:45 to 6:00 minutes per mile and some of this will be a bit slower.

*Speed Training for the week is noted by an Asterisk:

Day One

12 miles distance running at an easy pace of 5:50-6:30 minutes per mile in the a.m., then a light weight (20-25 lbs. for all but the bench press and it will be only 50 lbs.) workout session of three sets each of curls, military presses, bench presses, leg extensions, reverse leg curls and toe raises with a 20 pound dumbbell in each hand.

Day Two

Warmup of two miles, stretch and *then 4 x 1200 meters at 3:50 per mile pace (57 seconds per lap) and 800 meters recovery between each fast section. Cooldown with another two miles and patiently do a thorough stretching segment while the muscles are still warm.

Day Three

6 miles of easy distance and then a strength session in the gym of curls (three sets), military press (three sets), dead lifts (three sets of three lifts each), light leg extensions at a weight

the runner can extend comfortably for 8 repetitions before muscle failure begins and only down 30 degrees, as flexing thee legs with weight on them further than this, can over stretch the knee ligaments and does nothing for muscle increase. So, do (three sets with one minute recovery between sets), reverse leg curls, also at only a 30 degree curl up from horizontal (at a light enough weight to not strain the hamstrings, but heavy enough to produce mild muscle failure after 8 repetitions with three sets and one minute recovery between each set), toe raises to strengthen the gastrocnemius muscles (calves) with twenty pound weights in each hand, (three sets of 8-10 repetitions to mild to moderate muscle failure) and then abdominal crunches (three sets of 30 each) and finally a slow, steady stretching session focusing particularly on the quadriceps, hamstrings and gastrocnemius groups. Yoga is now used by many athletes and especially runners, to maintain good flexibility and calming of the mind and body. It is effective and helps in recovery from hard workouts and races.

Day Four

3 miles easy in the morning and 4 to 5 miles at a faster tempo based pace (5:25 pace) in the evening. Remember to stretch after warmup and immediately after every session of workouts.

Day Five

Warmup 2 miles, then *8x400 meters at 60 seconds each, with 200 meters slow recovery between each. Then, 8x200 meters at 28 seconds each, with 100 meters slow recovery jog between each. Cool down for two miles and then stretch.

Day Six
This is a six to eight mile easy run day and another light weight workout session with the same weights and sets as day one.

Day Seven
This is a six to eight mile day, with yoga or other meditative relaxation techniques of gentle stretching and practicing re-laxing the muscles and the mind from top to bottom.

Remember, this is the schedule for a high level miler. Developing milers will run their sections slower and most likely need more recovery between each fast section. Their base distance running should be higher, especially as they are developing and this is a time for maximizing lung volume and the other physiological effects distance training provides. The exception to this is the very young runner, as discussed. Every aspect of their training is much lighter. Over-training a young runner can do damage to them physically and can affect their desire to continue in the sport. This section is directed more to the adult, highly base trained athlete.

The miler also has to think of something else, in relation to training. In this author's opinion, there are no races harder than the 800, the mile and the 5,000 meters. None of these races allows for any 'down' time or long term planning during sections of the race. If there is planning, it must occur during the race itself and the ability to shift gears quickly is what must be planned for in training. The racer here must be able to make split second decisions regarding position, pace, surges and the time to go to 100% effort. Go too early and you will lose. The old saying, "train like you race" can only go so far, physically. In fact, if you have paid attention to this book, you will never put 100% out there in training. The purpose of training is to (A) give the athlete a glimpse of the pain and toughness, both mentally and physically, one will need to race extremely well and (B) to prepare the athlete through repetitive training for any acceleration and to hold any pace necessary, while racing. And that is it.

Tactics of the Mile Race:

If one watches an elite mile race event on a track, some common threads will emerge as the tactics of the race. First, the gun sounds and the runners complete the first two hundred meters in their lane. This is to prevent a pile up and a crash, as runners jockey for position. Typically, the first two hundred and fifty meters are used to establish initial position, without overtaxing the body. In very high level races from the mile all the way to the marathon, there are hired 'rabbits' to establish a fast or even record pace. These initial leaders are easy to spot, as they typically take the race out at a pace that will be difficult for most, if not all but one or two runners, to hold.

The rabbit's tactic is to pull the pack along to a fast time. 'Rabbits' are used because there is a natural tendency to let someone else take the pace, thus saving your race for a good kick at the end, to win. That never produces an impressive or record time. A record time in nearly every race ever run, has been the result of negative splits. This is the practice of running consecutively faster laps during the entire race, as mentioned earlier. This establishes pace no doubt, but also sets up both a new physical bar and mindset in the race. A miler who may never have believed he or she could run so fast, is suddenly caught up in a giant swell of emotion and a feeling of physical speed, without stress, never felt before. Hence, we see the live record race unfold. The best position for the miler, early in the race, is usually in 3rd to 5th place. That keeps the runner out of the pack, where collisions and tripping up can occur, yet does not force the stress of being the pace setter. As the race approaches 1,000 meters, the miler will best seek to start their move toward 2nd place. The modern miler is now strong enough to then move into a full anaerobic sprint for the last 250-300 meters of the race. I use meters here, but the difference between a mile and 1,500 meters is only about 109 yards. So, the tactic is the same. The ability of the miler to shift gears and call on fast twitch fiber within two steps is critical. Some milers recognize their competitors have more raw speed than they, so their tactic is to try to wear down the other runners with an early fast pace and try to hold on at the end. This tactic is seldom successful. The best milers understand and use that fine line that leaves them enough speed to sprint away at the end.

The Tactics of the Road

So, how does the normal road runner learn the tactic of racing? And further, how does one learn the tactic of racing distances on the road, where the split markers may not quite be where one expects them? During the Speed Phase, one important use of the track was to teach pace. Winning road races involves a precise knowledge of pace and when to accelerate away from the pack, with enough gas in the tank to hold off late charges by other competitors.

Well, now that I have you excited about running a particular race, how exactly will one position oneself through different phases of today's road races?

Intelligent 5,000 Meter Racing:

Many 5k races today are run on roads, in nearly all areas. Do not fret. There is a tactic system for this race, be it on the road or on the track. At the gun, it is not quite so urgent to establish position in the early stages of the 5,000. After all, one is going to run over three miles. However, there is indeed urgency to establish the contenders. This will become evident after the first six hundred meters. There will always be someone who darts out at a pace they cannot possibly hold, but resist the urge to chase this pretender. Instead, take the time to look around at the field. An experienced runner will always be able to identify those runners who are in true 5k shape. After that first six hundred meters, the field, if on a road, will spread slightly. This is for vision and also for positioning for the first turn. If the race is on the track, the field will line up a bit more, according to level of fitness. Use caution here. First, never believe a runner in tenth place at six hundred meters, cannot close the distance by the finish. Second, try to 'attach' yourself to a runner of just a bit more speed and endurance. Losing contact with the lead pack above 3,000 meters, is flirting with disaster, but there is still time to work your way back to the front. We have practiced this in training, during tempo and track workouts, so this concept should be comfortable to the athlete. By 3,000 meters, those who have properly trained their VO2 uptake and are also ready to activate fast twitch fiber, begin to sort out the pretender from the contender. Many of the best 5,000 meter runners use a series of surges, to drop all the remaining runners they can. There was a famous Ethiopian runner named Miruts Yifter, who used a series of 200 meter surges for the entire last half of the race, to drop all the runners he could. An acquaintance of mine, the great Craig Virgin, figured out Miruts' tactic and beat him with his own surging in the World Championships. Tactics can be learned, as you can see.

Most 5,000 runners will seek to have a smooth shift of gears and will try to run the last eight hundred meters faster than any other part of the race. I consider the 5,000 to be a very difficult race in sport. The last 200-300 meters will be completely anaerobic and it is not unusual to experience tunnel vision or a complete black out in the last meters of this race. This is fairly common but, if you experience it every time you race, see your physician to eliminate any other possible pathology one may be experiencing.

Outracing the 10k Competitor

The 5,000 and 10,000 are similar in the shifting of gears, but the 10k race requires the ability and training to use very high endurance and match it with tremendous speed for a longer period, obviously. The 10k elite race typically has many position shifts and a lot of these are meaningless. The field will usually have several runners who have nothing to lose by trying to beat up on the field early in the race. Additionally, especially in the 5 and 10k track races, there will be a team mentality if the race has an international field. The East Africans, as an example, have an unwritten code that says the younger, less experienced runners will be used to block and protect positions for the team favorite. It works well, but can be upset if a young runner decides it is his turn to take the older guy out. This situation can be used advantageously by the other runners to make the agreed pace chaotic and give them a chance to outsprint the field at the finish. This sometimes also happens in the marathon, but that race is so long it wears down the field to only leave the best at the end. The 10,000 is another race where having higher levels of fast twitch fiber comes in handy. There is a way to take out better runners, however.

Go out at your normal 15k pace and begin your acceleration at the halfway point. If you have trained well, especially during the Strength/Resistance Phase, you should have the ability to start tracking down your competitors earlier. And if you burn their legs out by four and one half miles, you can begin your final sprint. Work and train for this if you are not especially confident in your pure speed.

The Marathon Race Tactic

We have discussed the tactics of the mile, 5,000 meter and 10,000 meter race. However, we have not yet discussed the most accepted and efficient way of running the distance we have focused on, for most of this book. The marathon is not just another distance race, as many uncontrollable forces come into play with a race of this distance.

An excellent marathon can be derailed by the climate on the day of the race, as well as how prudently one has trained. The 'ideal' day for a marathon, is a temperature of approximately 40-45 degrees Fahrenheit, low wind and little to no rain. Unfortunately, there are not many 'perfect' days when this particular race distance is being held. The shorter races will beat the runner down less, when conditions are less than ideal. But, it has been as hot as in the nineties for some major marathons and it devastated the chance of good race times and has even been physically dangerous.

When we discuss the tactic to use in a marathon, it is very similar to the 10k or shorter races, but the shifting of gears is different. It is prudent to let most of the pretenders go, when the gun sounds. I ask my athletes to go out the first 5-6 miles a few seconds slower per mile, than they plan to average. This achieves two things. First, not as much glycogen is burned early, leaving more for the middle and latter stages of the race. I instruct them to set a pace within themselves that is comfortable, but not lagging.

At about six miles, I expect them to gradually increase pace for each mile after mile six, until they are at their race pace. Hold this pace through sixteen miles. As long as they are prepared, they can very cautiously put the hammer down and accelerate again. If they have conserved glycogen, they will begin their shift to higher fat burning ratios at the nineteen to twenty miles. With the Distance Phase and Strength Phase done as instructed, there will be more oxygen available to burn free fatty acids, without slowing too much. If the athlete pushes to the twenty-three mile mark like this, they will usually be looking at a negative split marathon and a fine race time. This is the guide. Experience will show the runner how to adapt to tough courses and non-ideal weather. Run smart and you will run fast.

Muscle Memory:

It is important to remember the body of an athlete is not in any way, comparable to the obese sedentary body. The athlete gets in shape much more quickly than the norm, after a layoff or an injury and comes back quickly when properly trained. This is a wonderful adaptation of the body and it is life long, if an athlete has initially trained into very good condition and maintained it for at least a few years. However, since the athlete begins to lose approximately 1% of gained fitness after going through the program, within 72 hours of stopping training, it is important to utilize even a low level of training when tapering. The downside of this muscle memory status comes when a good athlete becomes injured and comes back from said injury, too quickly. Highly trained runners are apt to want to dive right back in to hard training after this layoff. This can lead to another injury, sometimes on the other side of the body, as the runner is still favoring the injured side and puts too much stress on the 'good' side. After an injury has resolved, the runner should gently resume training for several weeks and not race during this time. As noted early in this writing, this is a lifelong sport and repeatedly injuring the body will eventually break it down for good, if intelligent recovery schedules are not followed.

As far as tapering for the marathon is concerned, the last 18 mile training run should be at least 10 days out from the race. Then, begin to cut daily mileages in the schedule noted earlier, before the big race. Keep well hydrated and eat the normal higher caloric diet one is usually following as a long distance athlete. This is the best form of loading carbohydrates. Don't drastically change diet to something like only pasta or potatoes. Allow your body to recover gently and build up glycogen by the sheer reduction in mileage and maintaining normal training diet. The last two days can be taken off or one may run a couple of miles to keep the jitters down.

Peaking
How Long Can It Last and Does Training Change?

The well trained runner can expect to 'peak' for eight to twelve weeks after finishing the Speed Phase. This means the runner can expect to maintain race form and race at high levels on a reasonable basis for this period, given races are spaced correctly and the race distance is considered. Of course, a runner who focuses on the 5,000 meter distance or shorter, can race more times than a runner who has pointed to half marathons and full marathons.

If we use the formula of one day's recovery per mile raced, we see this formula in a quite stark light. Milers race every week, during the Spring and Summer seasons and then work to peak again for the late Fall and Winter indoor season. Longer distance road racers can peak in the Fall and again in the Spring if they are smart about their training. They have a longer building Phase and therefore, shorter periods to race effectively. After this first year of seriously following the program written here, one can expect to be able to peak more often. The athlete will have a base to work from and instead of having to build in the Distance Phase for sixteen weeks, the athlete may only need eight weeks here. The Strength Phase will be able to be incorporated into part of the Distance Phase, as well. The Speed Phase will still be about six serious weeks, but the runner will be faster through that entire Phase.

THE FEMALE

THE TOUGHEST OF US ALL

As we have discussed these workouts primarily appearing slanted toward the male runner it seems, do not feel ignored if you are a female. These are examples, and the ratios of distance and speed apply to females, as well. They may have to scale back some of the mile repeats to three miles total, but they will also run them at the same fast ratio as the male and will grow into the same workouts as any male athlete. The female, in fact, may be able to recover from day to day, better than the male. They have essentially proved they are able to withstand more pain and have higher levels of overall endurance than males. As I mentioned earlier in this treatise, females can many times outrun males in ultra-marathons, even when both are equally trained. The female of our species is incredibly tough. They not only are raised expecting to have to push harder against their male counterparts to succeed but also, produce and raise children, in many cases. Though this is anecdotal to some extent, I have had the pleasure of coaching many females and interviewing even more. They analyze the issue, accept the pressure and complain less after hard workouts, than many of their male counterparts. So, if you are female and reading this, know that you are not only equally equipped to run to your maximum ability, as is an equally trained male, but you are many times more of a psychological force when the toughest parts of training and racing occur.

Nutrition for the Hard Training Runner (And anyone else, frankly)

The runner and actually everyone should practice a high nutrient density diet, with calories being only one part of this puzzle. I am certainly not an expert on nutrition, but my wife and I do try to take good care of ourselves and good nutrition is a huge part of our plan for not only quantity of life, but quality of life. We eat as many unprocessed foods as possible. Some of you may not eat meat and that has already been discussed in the earlier parts of this book. Personally, we do. However, we eat wild game and fish as our primary meat sources. Many may not have access to foods like venison, wild quail, even squirrel (one of the best meats you could ever imagine), rabbits and fishes. We try not to eat older deep, cold water species of fish, as the levels of mercury have been found to be higher in swordfish, large tuna and others. I believe this is a personal choice, however. But, we do eat a great deal of organically home grown vegetables and fruit. The less insecticides and chemicals used in these foods, generally the better.

However, all this being said, I do recommend a fabulous physician who is an expert on nutrition and is a runner and does other sports, as well. Her name is Doctor Ann Kulze. She is based in Charleston, South Carolina and has written many terrific books on nutrition, recipes for athletes and general health and is an award winning expert in her field. Please take advantage of her knowledge. I read her books and she is the real deal for training diets, foods to lower cholesterol and lessen the chances of heart disease and in addition to all this, the recipes and foods she recommends are great! Sometimes athletes think healthy eating means 'no taste' eating. Wrong. Look Dr. Kulze up on the internet or in most good bookstores. Purchase and use her books. She is to nutrition knowledge, what I hope this book is to training knowledge and practice. I have listed below, just some of her many great writings to make it easy for you. In addition to all of this, Dr. Kulze actually replies to emailed questions and need for nutrition help, personally. Now that is a huge plus! I do the same and if you are doing what we do for the right reasons, this is what you do.

Nutrition Books by Dr. Ann Kulze, MD. :

EAT RIGHT FOR LIFE:
Lovelace Health Plan-Wellness Council of America

Dr. ANN's 10 STEP DIET PLAN

Dr. ANN's EAT RIGHT FOR LIFE COMPANION COOKBOOK

Dr. ANN's WEIGH LESS FOR LIFE

Dr. ANN's EAT RIGHT FOR LIFE ON THE GO

Training is based in large part, on fuel intake. However, complex carbohydrates will metabolize into glycogen, the primary fuel of the runner. So will simple carbohydrates. Dr. Ann explains the reasons the athlete and anyone else, needs the higher nutrient form. She will be an excellent source for your training, to maximize your training and your overall health. She explains the need for more 'purely grown' vegetables and fruits and why we need fiber to keep us in fit digestive form. There may be another great nutrition expert out there, but Ann Kulze actually practices what she preaches, is involved in the sport and has the scientific credentials to back up what she recommends.

COMMON INJURIES AND TREATMENTS

All runners who are consistent in their training will suffer the occasional injury. This is a contact sport. Every step we take contacts the road, sidewalk, grass or a track. If we take approximately seven to nine hundred steps per mile and multiply that, times our weekly mileage, it becomes a very real issue to address. In this treatise, I have set the training program in definitive sections for several reasons. The first reason is to create or mold the body into an efficient and fast machine. The next reason, is to generate a program to follow that will be used long term, to build, strengthen, sharpen speed, taper and race, in that order. This is a program that can be repeated for most of a runner's lifetime if they choose. However, all bodies are not kinetically perfect. Therefore, injuries will happen. Additionally, we all have a built in tendency to try to achieve our goals more quickly than prescribed, at times. It is human nature.

So, what are the most common injuries to expect and how do we treat them? And what happens to our accrued training while we are dealing with an injury? The answers to these questions will be based on the type of injury sustained and the section of the program we are currently running. Injuries as a result of overtraining without proper rest periods, are what we see in most cases. The athlete will usually feel the overuse injury coming on and will, unfortunately, many times try to train through it. Some injuries will not require the runner to stop training, but treatment of the injury should be swift and consistent, even past the time the pain in the specific area is gone.

Rest is very important during training and important in treating an injury, most definitely. However, we must be proactive in treatment and not just think the injury will go away. This is seldom the case. The body usually breaks down in an area because of an imbalance of strength in antagonistic muscle groups, improper rest or because foot strike is improper. All of these situations can be corrected. Sports physicians and sports podiatrists are of great help to runners and most other physical activities when injury occurs. Do not be afraid to seek out a professional who is not only proficient in their knowledge of kinetics, but one who may also be a runner themselves. I have had a few physicians tell me they don't understand why people want to run. Those few are no longer in my phone contacts.

Since running injuries are usually coming to the surface for a few days or weeks before they become something that breaks us down for a long period, we can cut them short if we change a few aspects of our training and utilize both modern technology and understanding what we did differently to cause the issue in the first place and rework that part of our training. Some decrease in mileage is frequently involved in the healing process, but fitness can be maintained at the level the athlete was at, before the offending occurrence of injury. Some of the most common injuries we see are discussed in this section and the normal treatment for each is given, though sometimes the injury will require additional assistance to get the runner back in action. But understand this: running injuries can be healed for most, period. In my 53+ years of running and road racing and coaching, I have experienced most of these injuries and seen the rest of them. In each case, if the athlete was diligent in their aggressiveness of rehabilitation and consistently monitored their body to head off other injuries, they all were able to return to the training field. So, if you become hurt, do not despair. There is a fix for all the 'dings' we get in this sport. And all sports have injuries. So, let's look at some of the main injuries and how to fix them.

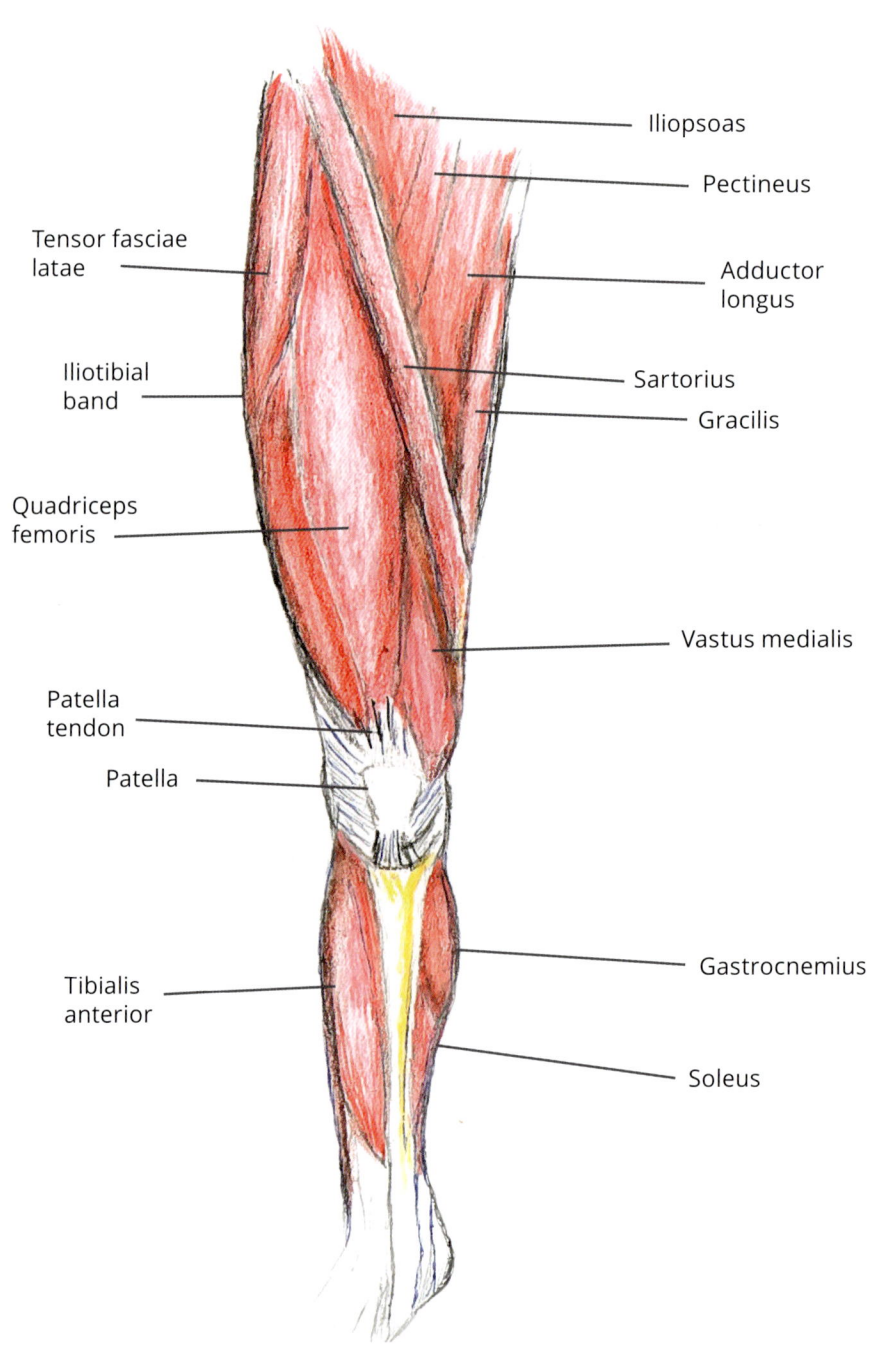

Iliopsoas

Pectineus

Tensor fasciae latae

Adductor longus

Iliotibial band

Sartorius

Gracilis

Quadriceps femoris

Vastus medialis

Patella tendon

Patella

Gastrocnemius

Tibialis anterior

Soleus

Anterior and Posterior Medial Tendonitis:

This type of injury is common, especially during the initial buildup Distance Phase and is commonly referred to as 'shin splints'. In fact, it is probably the most common pain complaint I see, particularly in runners who are beginning or are in the mileage increase section of this program.

Pain running down the inside of the leg, just below the knee and occasionally, down as far as the inside of the arch of the foot can be called shin splints or posterior tibialis tendonitis, or if on the outside of the shin, it is called anterior tibialis tendonitis. Note this is sometimes confusing, as another injury, plantar fasciitis can mimic the same symptoms in the area of the arch. In this injury, the tendon is not usually damaged, but the sheath of the tendon becomes inflamed as the foot strikes the ground and the foot over pronates, or rolls inward and flattens slightly to absorb shock. Pronation is necessary and normal, but over pronation stresses the medial tibialis tendon sheath and can cause pain. The pain can come from the sheath of the tendon sliding up and down over the tendon or the tendon itself, as it is being over stretched.

This condition is usually temporary, but should be treated with ice massage and the over pronation may need to be stabilized with an orthotic flexible arch. Anti-inflammatory over the counter medications may need to be used temporarily, but aspirin may upset the stomach and can also cause bleeding in capillaries, leading to slower healing. A reduction in mileage for a time may be called for to let healing speed. Moving to a soft, level surface such as grass may also help until the athlete has regained a normal gait and pain is gone. It is rarely necessary to completely stop running, but a reduction in mileage and speed is certainly called for. "Toeing off" is also occasionally associated with this injury, as well. If the athlete has decided to actively try to change the way their foot hits the ground and pushes off too hard, the tendon and even the Achilles tendon can be injured. Ice the area in a massage type movement from the knee to the arch, right after the run and again just before bedtime. Cooling the inflammation two or more times a day will be recommended for several types of running injury. Inflammation is a normal part of the body's reaction to the injury and is a protective mechanism to let us know we are in need of a change in what we are doing and also, surrounds the offended area with interstitial fluid to protect the area and supply more blood and healing constituents to the injured area.

Anterior tibialis tendonitis can be caused by one or more of several conditions. Over supination or rolling to the outside of the foot, hard toe off in speed work and running too many miles on dense surfaces such as concrete, can be the culprit here. Again, as in most overuse or foot strike instability issues, reducing the foot roll as it hits the ground and reducing mileage temporarily with a move to a soft, level running surface can speed the cure. And remember, though it may seem so simple, ice massage is a highly effective part of rehabilitation from most of these injuries. Continue ice massage for at least two weeks after all pain is gone.

The use of kinesiology based tapes can be of assistance in relieving pain and irritation when dealing with this type of injury and others, but be sure to read the instructions or better yet, use the advice of a skilled trainer who has a good knowledge of muscle and tendon physiology. These tapes are stretchable and help support the offended tendon sheath or muscle group. I personally, have had good results using these products. But again, knowledge of the direction a muscle moves and the supportive tendons and ligaments is a must, to receive consistent success. Most of these tapes come with a good set of directions, but there is no substitute for studying the body's muscles and tendons, so you will have an idea what area is becoming irritated.

Some runners believe just moving to a softer mid-sole shoe can cure these problems. Indeed, impact reduction is very important, but too soft a mid-sole can exacerbate foot roll and make the issue worse. Make sure you choose the proper shoe for your arch, weight, mileage and running form by consulting a professional in an independent running store or a sports podiatrist. Most of the time, employees in these running shops are also runners themselves and their involvement in the sport adds to their knowledge of the right equipment. They are more likely to understand the kinetics of foot strike, stride length and the issues associated with over pronation and supination of the foot. If you speak to a salesperson in one of these stores and they do not have a good knowledge of the shoe that is correct for you, keep looking.When the runner addresses these injuries or symptoms of adaptation quickly, they typically resolve and training can continue. If they do not, it is time for a professional to examine the issue. If ignored, they usually become debilitating and can completely interrupt the training regimen.

Metatarsal Issues

The human foot is highly complex and the toes (metatarsals) and their associated ligaments, bones and tendons can all become injured. One of the many possible injuries that can befall this area is inflammation of the areas between the toes, leading to neuromas between the toes. These can be very painful and it is recommended to have an orthopedist or podiatrist address the treatment of these. They are, like most running injuries, temporary, if quickly addressed.

These conditions are called Morton's neuromas and may require surgery in severe, untreated cases. However, good podiatrists are able to effectively treat this condition many times with orthotics, foot pads or prescribing a wider toe box shoe and the runner will be back in no time, though most likely with an orthotic to change the way the runner 'toes off' or launches from the foot. The podiatrist or orthopedist may recommend ice baths for the foot, also. Do not let this injury become chronic, as it can then require surgery to repair.

Additionally, injuries to the foot respond well to ice baths. They hurt like the devil when you first immerse your foot, but they soon become numb as inflammation reduces and circulation slows during the process. Ice baths are one of the most effective non-invasive injury recovery methods known for plantar fasciitis and other foot tendon injury cure.

The Knee and its Diverse Mechanics

Knee issues can be very complex, but with runners are, most of the time, another foot strike stabilization issue. Chondromalacia patellae or runners' knee is a condition that indicates the kneecap is sliding over the bursa sac under the knee upon foot strike. Several issues are at work here. There may be the foot stabilization inadequacy, inadequate quadriceps strength or the patellar tendon may be sliding over the patella and creating irritation, or a combination of all of these. This may involve the upper or lower tendon from the knee, as well.

Both, unless caused by specific sport trauma, such as lateral torque from soccer, tennis and less often but more severe, football, are easily treatable, especially if addressed in the early onset of symptoms. And then the athlete does not have an overuse injury, but a traumatic one. Runner's knee can be extremely painful. This I know from personal experience. In 1974, I decided to run the New Orleans Marathon, which was also the national championship that year. I made the number one mistake of nearly doubling my mileage within two weeks to hasten my fitness. By four weeks I was so crippled I could not run at all. Much less was known about the causes of this condition at that time. However, I read everything I could about the injury and finally came upon the cause and cure. I changed to a shoe with more stability, dialed back my mileage and iced, iced, iced. And of course, I missed the race. I was also at the Medical University of S.C., working in the Department of Laboratory Medicine and fortunately had access to excellent physicians and rehabilitative services. The condition resolved in about four weeks and I never had to learn that particular lesson again. The focus of rehabilitation was strengthening the quadriceps, alternating heat and cold, ultrasound treatments and reducing mileage for a time. This is a reason I and most others who really know the sport, never recommend sudden mileage and/or speed increases and keep the 10% maximum increase rule in effect when coaching athletes or in our own training.

The initial symptoms of this condition are actually pre-patellar chondromalacia, as there is little deterioration of the sub patellar cartilage and the causes of foot-strike instability, sudden mileage or speed increases in training, or obesity, can be controlled. Those reading this book are rarely saddled with obesity issues, but if one is beginning a new journey in life as a runner, then this condition can occur, but can more easily be treated, as well.

When the tendon above the knee and attached to the upper muscle, called the femoral quadriceps, is affected, there can be a different cause of pain, as opposed to the lower section of the tendon. Running downhill at a very hard pace on dense materials such as concrete, can cause micro tears in this tendon and associated ligaments. This is also a sign of weakness and imbalance in the femoral quadriceps muscle, as well as the other individual muscles in the area. Muscle balance is stressed frequently in this book and since slow distance training over- strengthens the anterior muscle groups called the hamstrings, it is wise to make sure good quadriceps strength is maintained and flexibility between the two groups is equalized. The quadriceps extend the leg and the hamstrings bend the leg, so there is danger in failing to work to balance the strength of the two groups. The same program of icing, running a reduced mileage schedule for a few weeks, strengthening antagonistic muscle groups and maintaining flexibility will resolve this issue, as well.[14]

This is one of the very few times I would recommend leg extension machines for runners. And with this type of rehabilitation, use extreme caution to only bend the leg approximately 30 degrees from level or straight. Bending past this point begins to put more pressure on the tendons and ligaments and less dependence on the muscle group the athlete is working to strengthen. This can stretch these tendons and further exacerbate the injury, instead of helping it to heal. Cease hard downhill running until the injury has healed and limit high density surface running. This means trying to use level grass or asphalt or a mix of the two, but no running on concrete for a while.

---

14   Mayo Clinic syc-20376113

Hamstring Tears or 'Pulls'

We tend to (erroneously) normally think of torn hamstrings as occurring only in sprinters or football players who use highly explosive power to accelerate. The fact is, this injury can occur in distance runners, as well. As discussed earlier, the cause is accelerating hard with muscles that are too tight or imbalanced from the antagonistic group (the quadriceps in this case). The Speed Work Phase is a prime time to have this severe injury happen, as we are running repeats from 200-400 meters with relatively short recovery times and have not stretched after the warmup or have not continued to be aware of quadriceps strength/hamstring strength ratios. A severe hamstring tear can be extremely painful immediately and can actually bruise the back of the leg. I suffered this injury in the 1977 Peachtree Road Race, when a spectator suddenly stepped out in front of me as I accelerated into the final sprint to the finish. The sudden swerve I had to make, coupled with the acceleration caused a terrible tear at the head of the hamstring and glu-teal muscle group. In the next two days, my leg bruised badly from my rear end to the back of my knee. I had to undergo six months of rehab and the injury finally resolved, though the scar tissue that formed around a small muscle called the piriformis, just at the base of my gluteal group, irritated the sciatic nerve for years. Continued stretching, foam rolling, massage, ice and time healed it. I also had electro stimulation which helped a great deal.

The athlete who suffers a bad hamstring tear will never forget the process of proper warmup and then stretching muscles while they are warm, before and after the workout. The above noted types of rehab I had, applies here to resolve the scar tissue and heal the injury, so there is no need to repeat it. Here is an injury I strongly recommend using kenisio-tape, to aid in stabilization. This relatively new product line works wonders on many areas of strained or pulled tendons, muscles or ligaments. Try it and follow the manufacturer's directions.

Light stretching as the athlete recovers, is mandatory, but do not force the stretch. Over stretching a hamstring to speed healing is counter-productive. Warm the muscle group, stretch and then ice. It may take a long while to repair this injury, but be diligent and you will heal.

Plantar Fasciitis and Plantar Tendonitis:

Runners with a low-arched foot can experience pain in the arch of the foot when changing segments of the program, having improper footwear or running too fast too soon. This can lead to plantar fasciitis, which can very quickly become chronic if not addressed aggressively. I mentioned earlier that shin splints can be misdiagnosed as plantar fasciitis or vice versa. One very painful sign of plantar fasciitis however, is a unique symptom. When the athlete awakens in the morning and steps on to the floor from bed, the pain in the bottom of the foot is usually severe in the arch area. It may subside after walking around awhile. The pain indicates the plantar tendon sheath has filled with fluid overnight and thus, the pain. The plantar tendon is usually not the problem, the sheath of the tendon is. If the foot strike on a low or very high arched foot hits the surface too hard without being ready for it (properly stretched or supported by good shoes or an orthotic), the tendon sheath can become inflamed. As fluid accumulates between the sheath and tendon as part of the inflammatory process of the body to protect injured areas, the runner may experience mild to severe pain on the bottom of the foot, especially when arising from that night's sleep. The pain may subside as the fluid is moved out of the sheath as the athlete walks around. However, the injury is still present and will get worse if not addressed. The pain may spread from the rear of the calcaneus (heel bone) to the metatarsals (toe bones). During rehab, ice water baths are extremely effective, but must be on a regular schedule and mild stretching of the metatarsals by sitting prone and pulling back the toes slowly and only to tension, not pain, can help. The full spectrum of orthotics, ice, stretching and reduced or temporarily stopped mileage, should be examined to keep this injury from becoming chronic. This injury can get worse quickly and heal slowly, so do not ignore it. In fact, you won't be able to ignore it for very long, as it will bring your training to a halt pretty quickly.

It is important to note that not only tibialis tendonitis mimics this injury and can present the same basic symptoms as plantar fasciitis, but bone spurs and nodules may, as well. To get an accurate diagnosis, a sports orthopedist or podiatrist should be consulted if this condition persists. Bone spurs and/ or nodules need professional care to be properly removed.

Achilles Tendonitis:

The Achilles tendon originates at the soleus muscle of the calf and terminates at the rear of the calcaneus. This injury can easily become chronic if not addressed right away and in sprinters, the Achilles tendon has been known to break or rupture. This condition occurs most frequently in sprinters, but can appear many times during the speed work phase of this program, even in marathoners. If the runner tries to 'run through' the injury, the tendon and tendon sheath can rupture.

Females frequently experience this condition due to the type of footwear many use, with high heels that tend to shorten the Achilles over time. When the lower heeled running shoe is applied, the tendon does not readily adapt, unless proper stretching has been maintained prior to and during training. If fast running is added in, Achilles tendonitis can develop very quickly.

This injury is tough to deal with. The 'cure' is moderate regular stretching of the soleus and tendon group, coupled with ice baths at least twice a day, immediately after the run or when coming in from any type of work. A heel lift may be prescribed by a podiatrist to temporarily take pressure off the rear foot area. If the athlete is not extremely aggressive and does not lighten the regimen, along with the icing, stretching and lifts, the issue can return. Fast running should be completely cut off during the rehabilitation of the tendon and should only be added back in after the runner has been able to train without pain for at least two weeks. Continue to use the lifts as prescribed by your foot professional. Don't become discouraged when dealing with this injury. Every good runner has had it at one time or another. Be diligent in your rehabilitation and gently return to your training schedule and you may never have this again. But, if one ignores the stretching routine for this and other injuries, they most likely will endure long term aggravation and disabling pain.

Iliotibial Band Syndrome:

The iliotibial band runs from the greater trochanter of the outside of the hip, down a small natural groove, where it then attaches to the anterior portion of the knee. This is another injury that appears to be more common in female distance runners, than males. The reason for this is most likely tied to wider hips in women and increasing mileage while either long training at a slow pace or fast running too quickly and not stretching the iliotibial tendon during the process. As the quadriceps group grows slightly at the onset of longer or harder training, the band can slide out of the groove and become inflamed. It is easily resolved, in most cases. The cure is a simple stretch. Stand parallel to a wall at arm's distance. While supporting your body with your hand against the wall, cross the outside leg over the inside leg and gently bend your arm to lean inward to the wall. You will feel the outside of the hip closest to the wall being stretched. One repetition should take at least 30 seconds. The athlete should do a minimum of five repetitions twice a day. The band will eventually stretch and return to the groove it normally sits in. Use a foam roller and a bit of ice massage to speed healing here. When using ice, try to apply it directly after the stretch and foam roller massage. Ice can be the runner's best friend. This iliotibial band issue is usually merely a product of increasing training in the first hard year of using this program. After the runner has the band properly stretched, it may never return. The anterior quadriceps muscles are growing early on during initial training, especially during the distance and strength phase and the band has simply slipped out of its groove.

Stress Fractures

Stress fractures can develop in several areas of the legs and feet of runners. A stress fracture is usually the result of overtraining without proper rest segments, racing too often, especially on dense road race surfaces like concrete or asphalt or in the case of femoral stress fractures, too much fast downhill running on dense surfaces. A runner can impact the road at well over 400 pounds per square inch and running downhill on very dense surfaces can up this to nearly 600 pounds per square inch. If you are a 150 pound male runner or a 110 pound female runner, calculate the number of steps you take in each mile and be amazed that the human body is tough enough to take this, even in ideal conditions.

Stress fractures mean time off, if you are smart. Continuing to push through a stress fracture can lead to a complete fracture. So, be aware and if you think you have developed a stress fracture, back your training down and move to a soft surface, or better yet, let the fracture heal. They are not un-common, but they are one of the reasons this program exists in distinct and planned segments. These fractures are much less likely to develop in well trained runners who are following the direction of not running too hard too soon and not racing until the musculature is ready. They are painful, whether in the foot, lower leg or upper leg and/or hip. They do not usu-ally show up on an X-ray until the bone has begun laying down calcium, which can be several days or weeks. In the meantime, the fracture can be growing worse. There are cases, though fairly rare, where a femur completely breaks in particularly, longer races like triathlons or ultramarathons. Newer scans can identify them, but the point is, this pain is a signal from the body that it needs relief. You will know, as you become a more experienced athlete, whether or not you are abusing the system. If you believe you have a stress fracture, get it exam-ined and let it heal. If you are on it early, you will be back pret-ty quickly. Newer types of rehabilitation for fractures involve electrostimulation that signals the bone to lay down more cal-cium and allow the bone to heal more quickly. And remember, the muscles are the support system for the bones and the bones are the framework for the body, so keep all aspects of your training and strength work up to a consistent level and all types of injuries will be less likely to occur.

Sartorius Strain

The Sartorius is a part of the quadriceps muscle group. (See front of leg illustration). It originates at the groin and crosses the front of the thigh, to attach at the anterior aspect just behind the knee. Strains of this upper section tendon occur most frequently at over striding at high speed downhill. It can become quite painful and due to its position, can be more difficult to treat. Gentle, and I use that word strongly, stretching can reduce scar adhesions and fast or any, preferably, downhill running should be curtailed during rehabilitation. Electrostimulation is effective for speeding healing and your rehabilitative technician can be of assistance here. To prevent it recurring, shorten your stride while performing on hills for a time and never allow the heel to strike hard as you come downhill.

Heat Issues:

I spoke of this issue from the very beginning and I include this in the 'runner injury' section, as it is the most dangerous injury, outside of direct trauma, that a runner has to deal with and should become knowledgeable about. The most dangerous potential injury an athlete can suffer is heat exhaustion or heat stroke, which can lead to death. Heat exhaustion is the first phase of severe dehydration and overheating. Heat stroke can kill a healthy individual or at the very least, leave them with chronic issues. Temperatures must be considered with two factors, when training. The actual thermometer temperature is only one of the factors that determine the recommended pace for the day. Humidity and high temperature together are the two factors that can endanger a runner's life.

We cool our bodies primarily, by evaporative cooling from our sweat evaporating from our skin. Trained runners have more capillaries to carry blood to the skin and thus, allow sweat to escape. The loss of 4% or more body weight during a run can signal real danger. The core temperature can rise to 104 degrees in this situation. Disorientation and weakness in muscles are a serious situation and should be immediately addressed with cool fluids and even cool water showers to bring core temperatures down. If you find you have stopped sweating, seek emergency medical care at once. Continuing to run with these symptoms can lead to a much more serious condition of heat stroke. Heat stroke symptoms are a core temperature of 105 degrees or higher and the body actually stops sweating. There may be chills, ironically, and the runner could collapse and die if medical attention is not immediately given. Runners with this condition may be cooled in ice water baths and IV fluids should be given with electrolytes. In both heat exhaustion and heat stroke, chill bumps may appear. This is a sign the body is struggling to bring down the core temperature and in both conditions, water and electrolytes should be given to regain cell homeostasis. Loss of electrolytes like potassium or magnesium in high levels and the fluid to transport and maintain these and keep the cells properly 'filled' can throw the heart into atrial fibrillation and death.

So what should we do to prevent this situation? Runners in the deep South have the most issues with these two heat-related injuries, but they can appear anywhere the temperature and humidity are high. If the humidity is above 60% and the temperature is above 80 degrees, the pace of any workout should be slowed by 10-20%. The runner will notice a higher heartrate even at slower paces. This is a sign the body is working harder to flow blood to the skin and provide as much evaporative cooling as possible.

Make a habit of weighing yourself before and after workouts. If you have lost 4% or more of your body weight during the workout, you should hydrate more and slow the workout. Taking in cool water or diluted electrolyte replacement drinks during the workout may help reduce this loss.

Even in cold races, the body is sweating to reduce core temperature. For instance, in 1979 I ran the Boston Marathon in very cold and wet conditions. It was sleeting and there was freezing rain at times. I weighed 132lbs at the starting line and 127lbs at the finish line, even though temperatures were in the low 30's. This is how severe the problem can be, especially if the athlete is running fast. So, be aware of this condition and take regular precautions to ameliorate it or stop the situation from occurring at all.

Heat and/or cold affect the ability of the hypothalamus to properly maintain body temperature. So, remember the body needs proper fluids and must not be overtaxed to the level it cannot operate all systems. If it is very cold at the start of a race or a training run, dress properly. Wear head gear and long running tights in particularly low temperatures. Gloves are also essential. You can always shed clothing during a run, but if you don't have it, you may get hypothermic.

In very hot weather, slow the pace, drink all the fluids you can and douse the top of your head with cold water, if necessary. All it takes is one bout with heatstroke to end your dreams.

Muscle Imbalance

In the earlier days of the sport, it was thought that running was all the athlete had to do, to achieve his or her potential. We know much more about the human body now. To become stronger and faster, we must ensure the antagonistic muscle groups are balanced to avoid the above discussed injuries, as well as optimize speed and endurance.

Many of the most painful injuries occur simply because the quadriceps and hamstring muscles, for instance, are not strength balanced and possess good flexibility. Some injuries are simply unavoidable, however, and it is a good idea to practice as much prevention as possible, to avoid even longer rehabilitation. This leads to the next section of preparation. Core and weight work.

Balancing the Body

In the earlier days and even in the 70's, it was unusual to see a distance runner athlete in the weight room. We now know that free weights or resistance machines and core abdominal work are all part of building a better runner. The previous sections, particularly as we built mileage and speed, included fairly light weights and high repetitions. Military presses, curls, 'flys' and crunches, some even with a three to five pound weight held against the chest, all contribute to good overall strength, more endurance and speed and most importantly, balancing the upper and lower body. You will not see 'muscle bound' distance runners, but if you look at any of the great runners, you will see definition in these upper groups. As I stated before, the legs turnover in unison with the arm swing, so going faster always includes arms with the ability to swing fast and for long periods of time, without 'tying up'. Your arms will swing as many times as the number of steps you take in a marathon. The abdominal muscles and diaphragm will also activate to help the lungs pull air in, so they must not be ignored in an effort to become the best runner you can. Make these exercises a regular part of your training regimen. Strong abdominal muscles also help to avoid lower back issues, as the anterior parts of the body are getting more attention during the normal training sessions. This leads to tight lower back muscle groups and the 'sway back' runner. The spine has a natural curve as part of our stature, but it is not meant to function well when excess lower back curvature creates pressure on the vertebrae. Strong abdominals counteract this unnatural compression.

Make sure you bring the groups along slowly, hence another reason for the Distance and Strength Phase. All balance should be attended to.

One of the reasons I believe early 20th century runners had shorter careers, is due to this lack of knowledge of training the body as a whole and avoiding 'fits and starts' in training. That is why we can have two and sometimes even three peaks a year, while avoiding injury. A well- tuned motor with a flat tire makes for a pretty poor overall race car. Remember this and don't flatten your tires while enduring to build the highest powered engine.

The Two Peak Year

The miler and the other distance runners should repeat the base conditioning phases twice a year and should only seek, to peak twice a year. And this is after completing the first full year of the program. The second year, the athlete responds faster to the individual sections and the sections can be done faster, thus providing a two-peak year. Base conditioning for the miler is similar, as we have seen, to the marathoner, but their overall mileage levels are lower and their strength and speed workouts are run harder. Trying to race year round is the way to become stale in a hurry. The body needs time off from this sport, but that does not necessarily mean completely shutting down workouts. After the usual eight to ten week peak phase, the runner should reduce both mileage and intensity of workouts. A way to do this without losing overall fitness is to go back to the first distance phase and run five to seven miles at an easy pace, five times a week, with two days completely off. Training is like any other job, only more fun. However, any job requires a period of mental and physical time away from the intense focus required to do the job well.

So, in the first serious year of training, we have used sixteen weeks building mileage and oxygen absorption ability, then eight more weeks increasing strength and eight weeks of speed training. That is thirty two weeks of training to get ready for eight weeks of top level racing, under ideal conditions. Forty weeks have been used in this first year for this endeavor. Notice, the first year will only have one technical peak. So, now, how much time should be used to recover enough to become ready to start the process over again? Usually, within three to four weeks of a full effort marathon, for instance, the athlete has relaxed both body and brain enough to be ready for the next buildup. So, even if the athlete uses a peak of twelve weeks, the next year is quickly upon you.

The second and subsequent years will see the athlete able to reduce the time spent in the individual sections and complete them in less than six months, thus opening up a 'two peak a year' system.

The muscle memory created from the first year of hard training will be of tremendous use. The runner, after some time off from competition, can start the distance phase at approximately 50 miles per week and reach 80-100 miles per week in three months, then spend six weeks in the strength phase and six weeks in the speed phase. Now, we are ready to race again in only six months from the start. This will allow for a Spring season and a Fall season of racing.

I have an athlete who has just reached that ability after a full year of paying attention. She went from a four hour and thirty minute marathoner, to a sub three hour marathoner and will now be ready again for an even faster marathon after rebuilding through the summer and early Fall. She should clip another ten minutes off her marathon time, without having to spend a full first year schedule of preparation. Her strength is much greater than when we met and she has learned to read her body. She is primarily a runner who focuses on distances from 5k to the marathon. She now knows she is not a miler, but she is a full-fledged distance runner.

The miler will be able to run more races with shorter recovery times, however. The athlete who trains for this distance will be able to have a serious Fall season and Spring season, without using as much base building time.

So, peaking is not only a matter of scheduling, but also a matter of recognizing the necessary recovery times for different distances. It has been said to expect to use the number of miles raced, as your guide to recovery for another full effort. For example, if a runner races a 5k at full effort, the runner should expect to take three easy days to let the body recover and cells restore maximum fuel, as well as repair of any micro-tears in tissue that may have occurred during a 100% race effort.

Even the Olympics try to use as much of this theory as possible, when scheduling the quarter finals, semi-finals and finals in distances from 800 meters to the 10k. There is only one marathon run in the Olympics, due to its incredible amount of effort required, so the participants will have to have already qualified at the Olympic standard before the race.

Recovery Times from Races:

Mile- 2 days

5,000 Meters- 4 days

10,000 Meters- 7 days

Half Marathon- 12 days

Marathon- 28 days

Recovery does not mean stopping training. Training should be reduced by half and speed work should be lightened to ½ to ¾ effort and repetitions should be cut in half for the distances from 10,000 meters to the marathon.

After the technical recovery, returning to normal racing and training should be resumed.

Year Two and Onward

When the second year of this program is begun, the phases will remain in the same order, but the speed and the ability to race faster and more often will be easier. The athlete will not be starting from scratch, so to speak and the mere fact the runner has a year round base established, will enhance the excitement of training and race goals.

The muscle memory and overall strength, coupled with experience, will provide the athlete with cues as to how fast he or she should be training, in order to increase speed in races.

For instance, in the initial year's Distance Phase, the athlete may have started with eight minute miles or slower. By the second year, that same athlete may be running most of their distance workouts at seven minutes a mile or faster. The heart-rate will be well within the 60-80% range, even while training faster. The body has increased the number of mitochondria in the muscle cells, there are more alveoli in the lungs for additional oxygen uptake, the left ventricle of the heart has increased in size, additional arterial and capillary pathways have been established and the mental focus and strength is now improved, so the athlete can handle harder and longer effort without having to think and concentrate so much about the workout. Remember the key, however. The first step out the door is the toughest, so consistency and scheduling will be necessary to perform at a higher level.

The Strength Phase of the second and subsequent years will feel more natural and the quadriceps and upper body will be stronger at the start, so the same effort will produce faster speed in the uphill runs and the weight work should become easier, as well. The weight work has been included in some form for most of the year, but the second year should not see a significant increase in the weight lifted or the number of repetitions. For instance, the athlete may be doing 8-12 curls with 15 pounds and with three sets, in the first year. The second year may only require 25 pounds for those same curls to achieve muscle failure at 18 repetitions. If a bit more weight is desired to achieve this effect, that is quite alright, provided the athlete does not turn the session into a session to increase muscle bulk. This is not the sport we are working toward. Remember, low weight/ high repetitions achieve our goals. The strength session will, however, include faster uphill running and more practice running downhill at higher speed. Here is an example to consider:

When I was training hard, it was not unusual to do 8-12 uphill runs of a half mile at 6% grade and at less than six minutes a mile speed. The downhills were run at nearly four minutes a mile and sometimes faster. At the base of the hill, there was a three minute recovery jog to return the heartrate to approximately 110 bpm. On the uphill sections, it was not unusual to have a two hundred bpm level, or a bit higher.

This was a workout done two times a week and a lesser effort workout of the same type running was done one other day. There was always an 'easy' day of running on level ground in between. That 'easy' day was usually 5-7 miles at 5:00 a.m. and 10 miles easy at 6:00 p.m. So, the concept of the strength run and workouts is relative to the condition of the runner. It is not your job to mimic other, more conditioned runners. However, is a great idea to run with a partner of equal or slightly better conditioning to maintain accountability and make each other do the workout on those lazy or busy schedule days. Runners seem to be able to find excuses for eliminating tough work-outs better than any other athletes I have seen. The runner that does not over think the day's session and 'just does it' will see better success. It is a shame to waste all the other work-outs because one does not appeal to the athlete. The best never question the day's work.

The Speed Phase of the second and following years will be thrilling. The main base of starting with mile repeats and eventually working down to two hundred meter repeats will be the same as the first year, but they will be much faster. The first year's mile repeats may have been six or seven miles per minute. The second year will see mile repeats of up to a min-ute per mile faster or better. Recovery times will come down, as well. By the time the runner has reached the four hundred meter repeats week, the runner may be going under five min-utes per mile for the now more conditioned athletes. The last two weeks that have a session of two hundred meter repeats, may see twenty-eight seconds or better for each one.

The second and next several years of the athlete's endeav-ors should see marked improvement in racing, faster recovery and the ability to peak twice a year, while still racing some ad-ditional lower effort local races. The body has an incredible ability to hold up better than the normal population, in ath-letes who have properly scheduled and listened to their body while training and racing.

The taper will always remain the same for the runner. There is no reason to change this part of the program. The recovery from races will improve, but it is up to the athlete to be diligent about not over racing, as this was discussed as one of the reasons many of the Africans and European runners seem to consistently outperform other athletes. The athlete who dedicates his or her life to maximizing results, will not have the same life as the sedentary socializing American. Their life will be better, period.

This is a statement that needs to be expressed. The American athlete, particularly runners, have finally begun to understand the somewhat Spartan lifestyle of other athletic cultures, is in large part the reason for their consistent success. We are too distracted by social media, alcohol and drug abuse (though athletes seem to have less of an issue with these here) and substituting other activities when our workouts should come first. In the last three to four years, our long distance runners have adopted a healthier type of program with great success and are now beginning to outrun the athletes they feared in past years. This program is just as relevant to the hobby runner, as the elite, also.

The Program in Review

As we have seen, there are many facets to becoming a good or great distance runner. We have learned how we developed into this machine of incredible ability in physical prowess, planning and evaluating a situation to mold ourselves into the best athlete in us. The program itself will always feature the same components of building endurance first, then strengthening the muscles we do not normally use. We then are ready to run fast in training, all the while keeping the body in balance by weight and core work.

We have come to understand the importance of rest as part of training, to let the body heal, rebuild stronger and decrease the incidence of burnout and injury.

One of the most important points we have learned is that the acceptance of high level dedication to this sport can come as early as a youngster or as old as you are now. Limitations are usually self- imposed.

We have come to understand that there will be some pain in workouts, at times and pain in injury, as well. No long term runner has ever escaped the last part and gone on to become great.

The now finely tuned athlete has realized that with intelligent planning, patience and study, he or she can race really well up to two seasons per year and use the time in between to recover and learn from our mistakes, as well as preparing to run the next year's seasons even better. The great John Kelly ran over fifty Boston Marathons in his 60+ year career. Bill Rodgers is now seventy and still competing in his age group. By the way, as I write this, I received a text from Bill telling me he had just won his age group in a large race, after coming off an injury. I have one athlete who is now literally running personal records at over age fifty and she has been a runner since she was in her thirties. I took her on as her coach two years ago and she is now focused and knows how to run the program. That is one of the beauties of this sport. With age group competition, one can run their entire life and race as long as their heart's desire. And if you never care to race at all, you will have achieved something very few people on the planet ever achieve. You will have become an athlete.

On Becoming the Best You Can Be

This section of editorial allowance is a statement on the general life of a runner. Runners are different, not just physically, but in the way they approach living. They desire to win at all things and usually outperform others in business, income, intelligence testing and are incredibly curious about the world and its people. I have been around both runners and non-runners all my life and have found the former seem actually happier. This, I agree, is subjective and may not have a great deal of scientific backup, but a person who is dedicated and driven enough to be the best they can be at the toughest sport on the planet, is more likely to enjoy the pursuit. And by this, I mean the pursuit of life. So, in conclusion, I hope this book helps you to become the best distance runner you can be. Seek to succeed and as Bill Rodgers said in his book, Marathon Man, 'chase butterflies' in your mind as you train. Happiness in this and all pursuits is a choice. Good running to you.

Terry Hamlin

GLOSSARY

ATP- Adenosine triphosphate is created from the intake and breakdown of foods. When a mole of phosphate is broken off, heat is created and energy is released to operate the cell, resulting in:

ADP- Adenosine diphosphate. Adenosine diphosphate provides energy for physiological actions, such as muscle contraction

AEROBIC- means with or in the presence of oxygen. Typically used to help slow twitch fiber and is the term for endurance paced running, in this treatise

ANEROBIC- means without the use of oxygen. Typically refers to fast twitch fiber operation and is the sprinter type cells. All humans have a combination of fast and slow twitch fiber

ALVEOLI- small air sacs of the lungs that function in the exchange of oxygen and carbon dioxide

ANEMIA- a condition marked by a deficiency of red cells and hemoglobin in the bloodstream. Produces pallor and weariness

ECTOMORPH- describes a lean body type

ENDOMORPH- describes an 'average' body type

GLYCOGEN- a substance deposited in bodily tissues as stored by carbohydrates and is a polysaccharide that forms glucose per hydrolysis

GLYCOLYSIS- the breakdown of glucose by enzymes releasing energy and pyruvic acid

HEMOGLOBIN- The 'heme'-bound molecule that transports oxygen in red cells

HOMEOSTASIS- Indicates a stable equilibrium between interdependent elements and/or molecules

HYDROLYSIS- a chemical breakdown of a compound due to reaction with water

HYPOTHALAMUS- the area of the brain, which among other functions, is responsible for controlling core temperature

LACTIC ACID- an organic acid formed in muscles as part of glycolysis and ADP conversion

MESOMORPH- refers to a heavy, stout body type

METABOLIZE- From Metabolism, meaning the chemical reactions within cells that provide energy for processes and synthesis (as in combination) of organic compounds within the cell

MITOCHONDRIA- organelles found in cells that aid in respiration and energy production. Highly trained cells contain more of these than untrained cells

MUSCLE FAILURE- the point at which the lactic acid level in the muscles becomes so high, additional repetitions of a particular movement are not able to be performed

MYOGLOBIN- a red protein containing 'heme' that carries and stores oxygen in muscle cells, it is a subunit of hemoglobin

OXIDATION- The process of oxygen combining with an element to change said element. In oxidation, as pertaining to muscles, oxygen must be in the presence of or combined with organic molecules to activate a process, such as in the synthesis and process of ATP to ADP for energy production.

PEAKING- the state at which the athlete has completed a total training system and is physiologically and psychologically at the summit of fitness

TAPERING- the process of reducing mileage and effort during the days prior to competition, to rest the body and build glycogen and nutrients to their maximum levels of absorption

TEMPO- is a running pace that equals approximately 85% of race pace. Tempo is used to train the strength systems of the body and is usually from 3-7 miles in length, during the middle of a workout

TESTOSTERONE- a steroid hormone that stimulates male secondary characteristics, produced mainly in the testes, but in small amounts in the ovaries of females and also in the cerebral cortex

VISCOSITY- as in the state of being semi-fluid in consistency, due to internal friction. Pertains here to rate at which blood can flow, from force per unit area resisting flow in which parallel units have equal distance. In simple terms, how slow or fast blood can flow under different situations and concentrations of molecules

INDEX

Research Materials:

Barron's Anatomy and Physiology- Professor Ken Ashwell, BMEDSC, MBBS, PhD- 2016 Quarto Publishing PLC, #6 Blundell St., London, UK, N7 9BH- 2016

The Hidden Mechanics of Exercise- Christopher M. Gillen- The Belknap Press of Harvard University Press, 2014

Who We Are and How We Got Here- David Reich, 2018 – Penguin Random House, LLC New York

Sports Physiology- Dr. Edward Fox- 1979, Saunders College Publishing, West Washington Square, Philadelphia, Pa. 19105

The Simon and Schuster Book of Anatomy and Physiology- Simon and Schuster, New York-1979

Origins- Dr. Richard E. Leakey and Roger Lewin- E.P. Dutton, New York- Rainbird Publishing Group Limited, 36 Park St., London W1Y 4DE, England-1977

A History of the Vikings- Gwyn Jones- Oxford University Press- 1984

The Mountain People- Colin M. Turnbull- Simon and Schuster Publishing, New York- 1972

Terry can be reached for questions, help or tips with your training or even personal one-on-one training at:
Email: Terry@coachterryhamlin.com

Look for additional training books by Terry, coming soon!